The Best
Men's Stage Monologues
of 2004

edited by D. L. Lepidus

MONOLOGUE AUDITION SERIES

A SMITH AND KRAUS BOOK

Published by Smith and Kraus, Inc.
177 Lyme Road, Hanover, NH 03755
www.SmithKraus.com

First Edition: August 2004
10 9 8 7 6 5 4 3 2 1

Cover illustration by Lisa Goldfinger
Cover design by Julia Hill Gignoux

The Monologue Audition Series
ISSN 1067-134X
ISBN 1-57525-403-4

NOTE: These monologues are intended to be used for audition and class study; permission is not required to use the material for those purposes. However, if there is a paid performance of any of the monologues included in this book, please refer to the Rights and Permissions pages 99–104 to locate the source that can grant permission for public performance.

The Best
Men's Stage Monologues
of 2004

Smith and Kraus *Books for Actors*

MONOLOGUE AUDITION SERIES

The Best Men's / Women's Stage Monologues of 2003
The Best Men's / Women's Stage Monologues of 2002
The Best Men's / Women's Stage Monologues of 2001
The Best Men's / Women's Stage Monologues of 2000
The Best Men's / Women's Stage Monologues of 1999
The Best Men's / Women's Stage Monologues of 1998
The Best Men's / Women's Stage Monologues of 1997
The Best Men's / Women's Stage Monologues of 1996
The Best Men's / Women's Stage Monologues of 1995
The Best Men's / Women's Stage Monologues of 1994
The Best Men's / Women's Stage Monologues of 1993
The Best Men's / Women's Stage Monologues of 1992
The Best Men's / Women's Stage Monologues of 1991
The Best Men's / Women's Stage Monologues of 1990
One Hundred Men's / Women's Stage Monologues from the 1980s
2 Minutes and Under: Character Monologues for Actors Volumes I and II
Monologues from Contemporary Literature: Volume I
Monologues from Classic Plays 468 BC to 1960 AD
100 Great Monologues from the Renaissance Theatre
100 Great Monologues from the Neo-Classical Theatre
100 Great Monologues from the 19th Century Romantic and Realistic Theatres
The Ultimate Audition Series Volume I: 222 Monologues, 2 Minutes & Under
The Ultimate Audition Series Volume II: 222 Monologues, 2 Minutes & Under
    from Literature

YOUNG ACTOR MONOLOGUE SERIES

Cool Characters for Kids: 71 One-Minute Monologues
Great Scenes and Monologues for Children, Volumes I and II
Great Monologues for Young Actors, Volumes I and II
Short Scenes and Monologues for Middle School Actors
Multicultural Monologues for Young Actors
The Ultimate Audition Series for Middle School Actors Vol.I: 111 One-Minute
    Monologues
The Ultimate Audition Series for Teens Vol. I: 111 One-Minute Monologues
The Ultimate Audition Series for Teens Vol.II: 111 One-Minute Monologues
The Ultimate Audition Series for Teens Vol.III: 111 One-Minute Monologues
The Ultimate Audition Series for Teens Vol.IV: 111 One-Minute Monologues
The Ultimate Audition Series for Teens Vol.V: 111 One-Minute Monologues
    from Shakespeare
Wild and Wacky Characters for Kids: 60 One-Minute Monologues

If you require prepublication information about upcoming Smith and Kraus books, you may receive our semiannual catalogue, free of charge, by sending your name and address to *Smith and Kraus Catalogue, PO Box 127, Lyme, NH 03768.* Or call us at *(800) 895-4331;* fax *(603) 643-6431.*

Contents

Foreword

There are sixty excellent monologues in this book, culled from the best plays published or produced during the 2003–2004 theatrical season. All are from published or readily available plays. Many are by playwrights with considerable reputations, writers such as David Lindsay-Abaire, John Patrick Shanley, David Rabe, Don Nigro, and Jon Robin Baitz. Many are by future stars such as Gina Gionfriddo, Seth Kramer, Brian Sloan, and Adam Bock. Most are monologues for actors in their twenties to forties, although there are some great ones if you're a geezer (like me), such as Pap from *The Reeves Tale* (hilarious) and Twain from *Pendragon* (mordantly funny, as you might expect).

Here are pieces written in a wide variety of styles.

In short, this is the best darn monologue book I could put together. I imagine you will find herein that great piece you've been looking for to use in class or for auditioning; but if you want some more options, I recommend Smith and Kraus' other fine collections of monologue books.

Now — go get 'em. Break a leg.

— *D. L. Lepidus*

THE ACTION AGAINST SOL SCHUMANN

Jeffrey Sweet

Seriocomic
Aaron, thirties

Aaron, a teacher, is talking about his recent trip to Germany.

AARON: I almost wanted to visit Bayreuth. You know Bayreuth? . . .
Otherwise known as Wagner Central. Did you know that when
he was a conductor — Wagner, I'm talking about — when he was
assigned to conduct a score by a Jewish composer, he wore gloves?
Yes. And after the piece was done, was finished, he'd throw the gloves
away? But he manages to get this place built — Bayreuth — this huge
opera house so they can stage his endless nutcase operas. So, years
later, Hitler — big Wagner fan. During the war, Hitler keeps the place
going full tilt — even when there are shortages 'cuz of the war — he
thinks it's the beating heart of the German soul or something. Including the orchestra, during the war, Jewish musicians. Yes, playing
in the pit. Wrap your mind around that one. You're a Jewish oboe
player, at the same time your relatives are being carted away, you're
playing *Twilight of the Gods* for Der Führer. How honored they must
have been by his applause. So — this is the part I love — when American troops liberate the town, some of the GIs look at this big opera
palace and say, "Hey, cool — a vaudeville house!" And they take it
over and put on a show. Every comic routine and number they can
remember — the Marx Brothers, the Ritz Brothers, Fanny Brice, Jack
Benny, Danny Kaye. Wagner's daughter-in-law hears about it, she
nearly has a heart attack. This vast, somber temple of high art being
desecrated with a bunch of jokes from kike comics. No, if there were
any place in Germany I'd actually want to visit, that would be it.

THE ACTION AGAINST SOL SCHUMANN

Jeffrey Sweet

Dramatic
Reiner, fifties

> *Reiner is talking to Paul, who is prosecuting the eponymous character for crimes he may or may not have committed during World War II.*

REINER: The barriers to Jews coming into this country were the product of anti-Semitism. And now, here you have this man Schumann. A Jew. . . . A Jew who did terrible things to other Jews. . . . There are some who feel that this can only encourage anti-Semites. "Look, you see, those Jews, give them the opportunity, they even turn on each other. Some of them — no better than Nazis." . . . Yes, but believe me, that's what some will think. And it will only make our job, our work on behalf of other Jews, that much harder. Nobody will *say* anything about this to us, of course, but it will influence the climate. And we're not talking only about the issue of Soviet Jews. Also the Middle East. The political rationale behind Israel is partially based on the idea of reparation. A homeland for people historically persecuted and brutalized. But if you announce to the world — See, some of them *helped* the Nazis do it to their own kind — . . . — is exactly what people do. After all, it isn't the story of the many that captures people's imagination. Four hundred die in an earthquake in Chile. Very sad. By next week, you've forgotten. After all, you can't focus on four hundred people. They're just a mass. Four hundred. Six million. Both big numbers. But *one* person can cast a long shadow in the public's imagination. Schumann has the capacity of casting such a shadow. As far as I'm concerned, what he did puts him beyond the pale. I will not argue that he is anything other than a monster. I talk to you not for his sake, but for the sake of others whose causes may be damaged because of the unhappy fact this man was born a Jew.

AFTER ASHLEY
Gina Gionfriddo

Seriocomic
David, thirties to forties

> *David is a TV talk show host, but he's about to move up to become
> a producer. He is talking to Alden, who has written a best-seller about
> coping with the tragedy of the rape and murder of his wife, Ashley.
> David wants Alden to take over as host of his show, which he in-
> tends to be about other survivors of violent crime against loved ones.*

DAVID: We need to talk about you and your future with this network. . . .

I'm going to Los Angeles tomorrow and I may be gone for a
while. I'm going to be covering the Shannon Smith trial for Court
TV. . . .

Soap opera actress. Murdered by a co-star. It's an awful story. The
judge won't allow cameras in the courtroom, so I'm going out there.
I'm going to cover the trial for Court TV and I'm writing a trial log
for *Esquire*. So I'm gonna be swamped. Meanwhile, I've had a promotion from the network. They've made me a producer. . . .

. . . They've made me the producer in charge of crime programm-
ing. I'm looking at a series of crime-based programs down the road,
but first thing I want to do is overhaul this show. It's not working. . . .

Alden, I'm on the women's channel. I'm here doing *Charlie Rose*
and that's not what the viewers want. They want emotion. So, we
change the format. We continue talking to victims, but we add color.
We do re-enactments of the crimes. The current thinking — because
it's a women's network, and because NBC is doing incredibly well with
this, uh, *Law and Order the Special Victims Unit* . . . the idea is to
shift the focus to sex crimes. Lot of interest in sex crimes right now.
Now, I'm all for it, but I can't do it. I've got this gig in L.A. and I'm
producing. So. I spoke with the network about you and they're very
interested in you taking over as host. . . .

. . . They've seen you. On *Charlie Rose*, on *Oprah*. We've seen your approach, your demeanor and we feel very good about it. I mean, I'll be honest with you. We did talk to someone else first. We spoke with another person . . . I don't want to name a name. He's the father of a murdered child. It's another high profile case. We sat down with him. A few times, actually. But this man . . . This is a man who — four, five years after the crime — is not recovered. The man has the demeanor of a rabid animal. He is angry and vengeful and that's not . . . that's not an energy we can work with. He's a warrior, and in his way he will make a difference. But he is not someone I can put on television five afternoons a week with rape victims. The guy made me uncomfortable . . .

. . . So new format: keep the victim interviews, limit the show to sex crimes, add re-enactments . . .

AFTER ASHLEY
Gina Gionfriddo

Dramatic
Justin, late teens

> *Justin's mother, Ashley, was raped and murdered four years ago. His*
> *father, Alden, has written a best-selling book capitalizing on the no-*
> *toriety of the crime. Justin is very angry and alienated, and he ex-*
> *presses this to Julie, a girl he has recently met.*

JUSTIN: Oh, I am ready and willing to lead the return to shame movement.
People are on TV eating bugs, trying to marry millionaires. Shame
is an idea whose time has come. Back. *(Pause.)* Now, you take September 11th. . . .

    People in this country don't know how to grieve. They're so . . .
estranged from silence and . . . reverence. Lisa Beamer — my God. That
woman makes my father look restrained. . . .

    . . . Exactly. That woman fucking trademarked her husband's last
words. She's on *Oprah* within a month, she's got a book out to co-
incide with the one-year anniversary. Who ARE these people? When
my mother died I was like . . . I could barely fucking dress myself. And
we had all these offers to go on TV and stuff and I thought well of course
we won't do that because that would be *insane,* but my dad . . . *(Pause.)*
Do you know who Christopher Collins is? . . .

    . . . After my mom died, he started contacting me. . . .

    I didn't know who he was, but my dad sure did. My dad was
fucking salivating that this famous writer was interested in me . . .
In us. Anyway. My dad tried to buddy up to him, but he didn't want
Dad. He wanted me to, like, go stay at his house in Iowa so he could
"get to know me" and write an article for a magazine. . . .

    . . . I didn't want to go. It was maybe six months after my mom
died and I was still . . . I was like barely a human, you know. But I went
cuz that's what my dad wanted me to do and . . . It was actually great.

5

We played video games and ate pizza. We went to theme restaurants with his girlfriend. I needed a friend really badly then because the friends I had were treating me like Quasimodo. No one could deal. So I start feeling good, like, I have a friend who can deal with this, with me. And then it turned. It was like all the good stuff was just fattening me up for the kill. All of a sudden we can't just hang out anymore, it's all creepy conversations like "Did you ever want to fuck your mother, Justin? You can tell me." And I'd be like, "No way, man. Not my thing. Want to go to Denny's again?" And he's all, "I have rape fantasies about my mother, Justin. Nothing you can say would shock me." So I call my dad, leave a whole bunch of messages which he doesn't get because he's in New York pitching his own fucking book. I am in Iowa with this increasingly creepy guy and I'm fifteen years old. This guy is saying things like . . . "Violence gives me a hard-on. Does violence give you a hard-on?" Finally, I go to bed at, like nine o'clock just to get the fuck away from him. End of the story? His girl-friend crawled into bed with me and we had sex. I lost my virginity. Guy stopped speaking to me. I charged a seven hundred dollar flight home on my dad's credit card, kicked in a window in my house and just stayed . . . by myself til he came back from New York. . . .

It's fine. It's not, like, Bosnia or anything. But it's fucked up! The point is just . . . My mother was murdered. Horribly. I don't know what the aftermath of that is supposed to be, but I don't think it's supposed to be . . . a book and a TV show and a rap song and a girl in my room. It's like we've lost the truth of it, we've buried her pain under all this . . . junk.

ALONE IT STANDS
John Breen

Dramatic
Tom Kiernan, forties to fifties

> *Kiernan is the coach of an Irish rugby team. He is talking to one of his players, as he is exercising, about what it takes to be a great player.*

KIERNAN: When you are an athlete in peak condition it doesn't take a lot of work to maintain that. But to break through your own personal plateau and reach an altered state of fitness, where your body is so attuned that even your perceptions are sharper, one must have qualities that are rare even among athletes. It's all about pain, Seamus, about accepting excruciating pain as part of the fabric of your everyday life. Your body doesn't feel safe working this hard. It sends out signals to this effect. Your lungs ache, legs feel tired and heavy, your head feels tight, mouth dry. You ignore it, accept it. Now your body gets more persistent. Stop. Pain. Stop. Pain. Stop. This is when most people do stop. But if you look at great athletes in their prime, at the final stretch of the fifteen hundred meters at the Olympics, if you look at the faces of the runners as they come down that final straight, or at the face of a wing forward making a break for the line late in an International — the look on their faces isn't elation, Seamus, it's agony.

ALONE IT STANDS
John Breen

Seriocomic
Russ, twenties to thirties

> *Russ is a star player on a New Zealand rugby team about to play*
> *an important match with a top team from Ireland. He is here talk-*
> *ing to two other players.*

RUSS: What the fuck do you two think you're doing? . . .
　　　　Bollocks, you should have been warmed up a half an hour ago.
I said fifteen hundred press-ups before ball work and I meant it. . . .
　　　　(Robertson sighs.)
　　　　All right, Wilson, that's an eighty dollar fine. . . .
　　　　Audible sighing. I won't stand for that. You lot are walking around
like film stars; posing for photographs, autographing sweaters. . . .
　　　　Don't split hairs with me, boy. Complacency is our enemy, boys.
Now I keep hearing about training runs against regional teams before the main event? *(To Mourie.)* That is not what the All Blacks are
about. You consider yourselves as the pinnacle of rugby talent. You're
here to give the locals a lesson in how it should be played. Chase a
few girls, have a few beers, a nice easy run against a bunch of local
yahoos, all very nice and friendly. You know what these local yahoos
see when they look at you. *(Pause.)* Anyone? *(Pause.)* They see the
most desirable virgin in all of rugby. Pure. Unsullied by defeat. And
they want you. Look at how we're pissing about! You know what happens to virgins who piss about? . . .
　　　　They get fucked! If you girls don't wake up and rediscover your
pride and dignity that's what Munster will do to you. *(To Robertson.)*
They nearly beat us in '74, yeah? Do you want to go home and say
"We lost. They beat us. We let them."? . . .
　　　　No. We travelled around the world to get beaten by a bunch of
scrawny Irish peasants? Now they think we're arrogant. Because we

are the best. And they hate us. They want to grind our noses in defeat. Now, they will tackle like demons, they will ruck and scrum like wild animals. They're fast and unpredictable. *(Beat.)* But they're small. If we don't let them have the ball they can't score. We control the game up front. No fancy stuff. A good hard clinical performance, and we will hammer these poor bastards. And, Wilson, any more talk of mead or Bunratty women — . . .

— and I swear I will personally deflower you myself.

ANCIENT LIGHTS
Shelagh Stephenson

Comic
Tom, twenties to thirties

*Tom is an American movie star here being interviewed on British
TV about his latest film.*

TOM: Thank you very much . . . Thank you . . . Hey, who says the British
are tight-assed? Am I allowed to say that on TV? Excuse me? . . . My
pleasure, totally, it's great to be here, Michael. I love England. I did
a couple of years here as a student and I totally fell in love with just
about everything. That whole experience has kind of resonated down
my life, you know? I always knew I'd come back, it was just a matter of when . . . I mean like, to stay a long while . . . maybe take a
house . . . Excuse me? . . . I'm over to see some old college friends
actually . . . we were like the Three Musketeers, shared a house for
two years, me and two women, knew each other inside out. Still do.
It's good to get together occasionally . . . I remember this thing from
like twenty years back for some reason, I've never forgotten it. I was
walking along a riverbank in England this time, on a beautiful breezy
summer's day, and there was an old house right there on the tow path,
with chestnut trees and honeysuckle, and roses falling over the gate,
and on the side of the house, high up, near the roof, was a wooden
sign that said "Ancient Lights." And it struck me like a poem, like
an echo of something long gone, kind of pagan and all tied in with
this old, old river and this tumbling greenery, and it's just, I guess,
kind of stayed with me, it's kind of reverberated inside of me all these
years, you know . . . Excuse me? Sorry, sorry, I just got in from L.A.,
so I'm a little tired, a little slow on the uptake. Have you tried mela-
tonin? Some kind of mineral or vitamin or maybe it's an herb. I don't
think it's chemical. Something to do with your pineal gland. It kind
of takes the edge off jet lag. I'm double dosing. Maybe I should triple

dose. There's some other thing where you shine a light at the back of your knee, d'you know if that works? But right, yeah, the weather . . . well . . . it's pretty scary after California, but I kind of like it. Real snow. I haven't seen snow for, like, ten years. I mean I can't believe it. Real fucking snow . . . Well, what can I say?

Big Sky . . . yeah . . . it did pretty good business in the States, so we're hoping, you know . . . Right, I play Joe Washington, he's a paraplegic forensic guy whose marriage is in a mess and he's drinking too much and there are some really weird killings going on and you know he gets to thinking . . . I don't know, basically I play a cripple in an Armani suit who gets to have sex with a lot of women.

BIRDY
Naomi Wallace

Dramatic
Sgt. Al, mid-to-late twenties

Al is talking to his pal, whom he calls "Birdy" because of his child-hood fascination with birds. Both are in a hospital — Al, to recu-perate from wounds he suffered in battle (World War II). Birdy is catatonic from shell shock.

SGT. AL: Look, Birdy. This guy's giving me a special chance to feed you. Open up! . . .

I know the whole thing is damned undignified but what's the difference? Either he feeds you or I feed you. If you're going to pre-tend you're a stupid bird, at least be consistent . . .

OK. Let's try it like real birds. You don't like the spoon because you're a bird, right? Then I'll chomp up some of this mush and pass it to you, just like a true-blooded tweetie feeds her chicks, right? Isn't that what you used to do with your birds? *(Beat.)* Birdy! . . .

It doesn't matter, does it, Birdy? Isn't that what I heard you say more than anything else. According to you, nothing mattered. I'd be burned up about something, at school, or your mother, or my father, and you'd say: It doesn't matter. But then what did? Besides the birds? *(Beat.)* Those fucking birds. When you were in hospital after you fell off the tank, you thought your birds flew away cause no one fed them. Your birds didn't fly anywhere. Did you know that? I came by your house that week one afternoon when you were laid up, to check on your birds. I found your mom shoveling them into a garbage can; she poisoned them. All twenty-five of them. That was the only time I ever lied to you. *(Beat.)* You know what's going to happen to you? They're going to keep you locked up like this all your life. I bet there are hospitals all over the country filled up with war nuts. *(Beat.)* Birdy. I know you're not hurting anybody. Trouble is, if they let you out, you'll probably go jump off some high building or try to fly down a staircase or out a window or something. What the hell, if that's what you want to do they should let you. You never were dumb, Birdy. Most things you did made sense. In a way. But I don't know about this stuff. Are you crazy, Birdy?

BIRDY
Naomi Wallace

Dramatic
Young Birdy, midteens

Birdy is obsessed with birds — hence his name. Here he is talking to some of his caged birds.

BIRDY: It's hard to know you're dreaming unless you catch yourself doing it. I was working in one of the flight cages when it first came to me. I'd put all the birds into the breeding cages and there were already eleven nests built and over thirty eggs had been laid. Everything was going beautiful. I got into one of the flight cages to clean the floor when suddenly I realized I'd been in this cage but my view of the cage had been different; it was the view of a bird. At first it was as if I were thinking it, daydreaming, then I knew I was remembering the dream. And I could remember many nights of dreaming; it seemed to go back a long time. *(Beat.)* In my dream, I'd been living in this flight cage with the other males. I could talk to them. I made sounds like a bird. I ate seed. In my dream, in the cage, I learned to fly the way I've always wanted to fly. *(Beat.)* I'm turned upside down. The days seem more like a dream than the dream. The realest thing is the dream and the next real thing is watching my birds. And in the dream I see myself sitting on a chair with binoculars. I can't see my face but I can look at myself all I want. Me, out there, doesn't seem to know about me in the cage, hanging on the wire. How can I see myself in two places at once? *(He opens his shirt and feels his body.)* One thing I know now is that flying isn't anything like swimming. It isn't all pushing down, catching air under the wings and pushing against it. There's a feeling of being lifted from the top, of moving up into an emptiness. *(Birdy spins in his squat.)* I'm no longer a boy.

THE BLACK MONK
David Rabe

Dramatic
Kovrin, thirties

*Andrei Vasilich Kovrin is a scholar and idealist. He is here talking
to Tanya, the daughter of the man who raised him as his own son.*

KOVRIN: I've been thinking all day of it, and growing more and more frustrated. It's this book — the one I was looking for. It contains a legend that I — . . .

I can't stop thinking about it. . . .

I'm fascinated by it and I feel the need to — but I can't find the book it's in. I've looked everywhere. . . .

Of course, you could have [heard of it], but it's unlikely, because I have the feeling the source is esoteric. But it tells how one thousand years ago a monk, dressed in black, walked into the desert in Arabia. He walked over the sand, up and down the dunes and in those very same minutes, fishermen, hundreds of miles away saw a black monk gliding over the surface of a lake. *(At the piano, someone plays.)* This second monk was a mirage. Now don't try to apply the laws of optics, because the legend pays no attention to them. Just listen to the rest. The mirage of the monk at the lake produced another identical mirage above it, and from that one came another, and on and on so that almost instantly, the image of the black monk was sent endlessly from one level of the atmosphere to the next resulting in the Black Monk being seen in Africa and in Spain. There were Italians who saw him. People in the Far North. And all at the same time. And then he sailed right out of the Earth's atmosphere into the heavens. *(This leaves him gazing up and out at the star-filled sky.)* And there he has roamed ever since, never finding the right conditions that might allow him to fade away. At the moment he might be seen on Mars, or near a star in the Southern Cross. *(Glancing at Tanya who gazes skyward.)* But the main point, the heart of the whole legend is that exactly one thousand years from the day that monk first stepped into the desert, the mirage will come back to the Earth . . . *(Once again he studies the heavens as if expecting to see the Black Monk.)* . . . and people will see it. According to the legend, the thousand years is coming to an end. So we should be expecting the Black Monk any day now.

THE BLACK MONK
David Rabe

Seriocomic
Kovrin, thirties

Andrei Vasilich Kovrin is a scholar and idealist. He has just been talking to Pesotsky, a renowned horticulturist and his adoptive father. He then turns and directly addresses the audience.

KOVRIN: The orchard. Of course he's worried about the orchard. He loves the orchard. It's his work, and — *(He stops, steps toward them.)* Marry Tanya? Did he mean it? The way he suffered about who would inherit his farm; the way he struggled to know its fate. You'd think he was in a war even here on this idyllic site. So is it that way for all men today? We must all be ready to defend ourselves, always ready for battle. At the university, they say to me, "Is that your idea That! You would like us to consider that!?" And they are openly disgusted. *(Even more directly to the audience.)* Do you have an idea? What is your idea? We have ideas. What else is in our heads? And so I must answer them, "Yes. It's mine. It's what I have. It is my thought." And if they're right? And it is disgusting. Is it not still mine? *(Freezing, annoyed with himself.)* No, no — no more thinking about orchards. *(Grabbing and ringing a servant's bell.)* I need to work. I need to find that book in which the legend is described, so that I can more fully — *(Again, he freezes and moves to the audience.)* Marry Tanya? Did he mean it? Did he actually mean it? *(Once more annoyed.)* What am I doing thinking about such things? After what happened in that field. After what I saw. No, that is what matters. That is . . . Perhaps if I just close my eyes and think, the name of the book will come back to me. *(Closing his eyes, standing very still.)* If I close my eyes and think about the legend, about the Monk. *(After a beat, his eyes still closed.)* Do you know what? Thinking like this seems to dismiss all need to find the book. It's as if my questions have been answered when they haven't. Yes. Thinking about the Black Monk suggests that thinking about the Black Monk is all I need to do.

BUCKET OF MOON
(from *Special Days*)
Seth Kramer

Dramatic
Jess, late twenties to forties

> *Three days after the 9/11 tragedy, Jess, a guilt-wracked NYC fire-*
> *fighter, turns to his pregnant wife, Dee, while he tries to come to*
> *grips with the horror of working at Ground Zero.*

JESS: We used to — God, I haven't thought about this in years — Brian
and I, growing up — we used to play "King of the Hill" on the roof
of our old apartment building in Jersey City. *(Laughs.)* Pair of freakin'
morons we were. Mom — Jesus — she found out and went ballis-
tic! First and only time she ever took a belt to either of us. Still, nothing she did could stop us from going up there. *(Beat.)* By the time
we'd turned thirteen it was the only place to be after midnight. Brian
and I — We'd sit up there and pass a joint back and forth and stare
out over the water at the Trade Towers, watching the lights blink in
and out half the night. Talking about what we wanted to do with our
lives, where we wanted to travel, becoming firefighters, stuff like that.
    (Beat.) I grew up on that roof. Grew up seeing those towers every
day. Every Day. They were like the moon, you know? Like the moon
or the ocean or a mountain. Something so vast and — and completely . . . I don't know. *(Pause.)* Permanent. *(Beat.)* Now I go down
there and it's just — *(Beat.)* I get in that line and I start doin'. Bucket
after bucket. One after the next. Like a bunch of men trying to move
Everest one stone at a time. And I don't think. CAN'T THINK about
anything. I'm just there — Another pair of hands in a long line. *(Beat.)*
And before I know it, two hours have gone by, and then four and
after a while the sun's coming up or going down and all I've done,
more times than I can count, is just pass that bucket. Pass that bucket.

And always — ALWAYS — it gets passed back to me just as full as it was the last time. *(Pause.)* Nothin'. *(Beat.)* Nothin' we do matters now. We don't save any lives. We don't rescue anyone. Most of the time we don't even find any body parts. Just rubble. *(Pause.)* Just buckets.

CATS CAN SEE THE DEVIL
Tom X. Chao

Comic
The Talking Cat, any age

> *The Talking Cat appears in the puppet show that makes up the first part of the play. In the productions to date, a cat plush toy was manipulated like a hand puppet while the actor playing Tom (The Narrator) provided the voice of The Talking Cat. For a class or audition, an actor may present the monologue without an accompanying cat toy or puppet. The Talking Cat's voice should be deep, hoarse, and "blown-out." A New York City or New Jersey accent may be used if desired. Here, The Talking Cat attempts to educate the audience by debunking various myths about cats.*

THE TALKING CAT: *(Musing.)* Awww! You want me to talk . . . oh, all right! *(Clears its throat noisily.)* Good evening, I'm a cat. I'm a real cat; I'm not a stuffed animal. I'm here tonight to dissuade you from a lot of notions you may hold about cats; I'm gonna debunk a lot of myths. *(Pause.)* Cats aren't what people think we are. We aren't clean and neat. We're filthy, disgusting creatures, covered with lice, vermin and stray bits of our own fecal material. *(Fast.)* We are profligate, dissipated, undisciplined, hard-drinking and mentally ill. *(Normal again.)* We breed wantonly and abandon our kittens. *(Intimately.)* One old wives' tale about cats is true. We can see the devil. Yes. It's true. When the wind is howling outside and you see us suddenly start and hiss at some unseen presence in the corner by the china cabinet, that's a sign that we're seeing the devil. We are receiving our commands to go and commune with Lucifer at our secret meeting place. In your backyard. Behind the shed. We are familiars of Old Scratch himself. *(Normal tone.)* You know, a lot of people think that my anti-cat statements play right into the hands of people who hate cats, and also into the hands of . . . dogs. Some people even call me an "Uncle Tom . . . Cat." *(Angry.)* But I say fuck it! Fuck it! I'm here to speak the truth, not reinforce stereotypes. *(Subdued.)* Well, that's pretty much all I gotta say.

DEBT
Seth Kramer

Dramatic
Dwight, twenties to thirties

> *Dwight, a gay man, is recording a heartfelt apology to his former lover who refuses to speak to him.*

DWIGHT: You won't talk to me.
> *(Pause.)*
> I don't know what else to do. You won't return my phone calls, or open the door when I buzz, or even meet me somewhere. This was the only thing I could think to reach you. This — talking into this stupid machine. Trying to explain to IT what I should be explaining to you — and if you would just . . . I mean, why won't you just talk to me, Scott? Why are you shutting me out? It's not right.
> *(Beat.)*
> Actually, you know, I almost erased this. Again. This is like the twentieth time I've started over. It's hard because, I record one of these messages to you and then, I listen to it and it all sounds so . . . I don't know. So wrong. And I want so badly . . . am trying so hard to figure out what it is that I need to say to you . . . the RIGHT thing to say to you that'll make it better.
> *(Flaring.)*
> God, I'm so tempted to just tape over all this with music and just get rid of the idea entirely. I even put the Top 10 country hits of the year on the other side. Because I know you hate country. I'm so fucking mad at you for shutting me out like this. I'm sorry, but I am.
> *(Beat.)*
> I wanted to but I couldn't.
> *(Pause.)*
> I'm just going to apologize. I don't know if you can accept that

from me or not but I realize now what I did hurt you. I think I understand what happened. What you're feeling . . . But that's also part of the problem. Isn't it Scott? I know what I THINK it was but since you won't tell me, won't even talk to me, I may never know if I'm right. But I think I do. So I'm sorry. I didn't know how you'd react.

(Beat.)

I thought you'd like it. Kill me for wanting to do something for you I thought you'd like. I let myself forget how little I actually knew you. I was so sure we had this connection — that I understood . . . But in the end I was just doing the things that I enjoyed. I wasn't listening to you. And now you won't speak to me.

(Beat.)

I don't know, I had to try and reach you somehow. Mail this tape to you. Slip it under your door.

(Beat.)

I miss you, puppy. Every day — every day before work, I go by the park just hoping that you'll be there . . . finally ready to talk or fight or even hit me. Anything except this — shutting me out like this.

(Beat.)

Maybe you haven't even listened to this. Maybe you threw it out the moment you got it. My message in a bottle.

(Beat.)

But I sent it to you, Scott. I sent it.

DIRTY STORY
John Patrick Shanley

Dramatic
Brutus, forties

> *Brutus is a successful novelist, here talking to Wanda, a young novelist who has asked to meet him.*

BRUTUS: Are you a frog? Do you want to have ideas that legitimately unspool from within? Or are you content to sit on your lily pad believing that you are having thoughts when what you are actually having are belches caused by swallowing undigested chunks of culture?! Originality is not for frogs croaking in chorus. I'll tell you something real. Originality is soul. Every era has its words. There's a word around these days. Authenticity. People are looking for authenticity. It's just the latest word. People are looking for their souls. They climb mountains looking for it, go into the desert, mingle with the destitute. Enter tombs. You think I'm crazy? You've just joined the villagers chasing Dr. Frankenstein's monster up the hill. There was a movie! And no one understood it. Those villagers were the Nazis. And what was the Creature? The Creature was Soul. "It's monstrous! Kill it!" Maybe they were right. But they started a fire in the castle that's burning still. That's it. I've gotta go.

DIRTY STORY
John Patrick Shanley

Dramatic
Brutus, forties

> *Brutus, a successful novelist, has lured Wanda, a wannabe writer,*
> *up to his apartment where he plans either to teach her a lesson or*
> *reveal that he is in fact some sort of psychopath.*

BRUTUS: Hello? Hi. You fainted. The *Moonlight Sonata.* So now you know
something. Now you've had an experience. Something concrete.
You're in the soup. You've been living in your head too long. Don't
you feel better? *(She looks at her stomach, realizes her didn't cut her.*
She whimpers with relief.) No, I didn't cut you up. Actually, WE'VE
had an experience. That's right. Now there's a WE. We have a rela-
tionship. There's a bond. Maybe I'll give you a nickname. Any sug-
gestions? Good idea. Nipples. Let's just put some clips on those. One.
And two. *(He's put clips on her nipples.)* But back to Pauline. She's
tied to the tracks. SHE'S not gagged. What do you think she really
says to the Villain once she sees the train in the distance? The danger jacking up each moment. At first, certainly, she appeals to his
humanity, his decency. But when that falls flat, she, undoubtedly speaks
to him as a Man. She offers herself to him. Of course she doesn't mean
it! She's just trying to save herself. But as the approaching train's vibra-
tion starts to rage like a hyena through her body, and the concept that
this guy is her only hope solidifies into certainty, doesn't it seem likely
that her pretense of lust would terrify down into lust itself? That the
fiction of her civilized character would start to fall apart? That she
would begin, in the savage grip of self-interest, to genuinely experience a ravenous desperate desire to please this man, to indulge this
man, if only he will save her? She makes promises. Terrible, beautiful promises . . . And while she says these things, her voice, com-
peting with the train, rises in intensity, in sincerity, in depth of

conviction. Until finally, she breaks through. And she offers to die for him. She loves him. She loves him so much. She is so utterly committed to his will. She is content to die for him beneath the wheels of the oncoming train. All she asks is a single kiss. And at that moment of perfect subjugation, the Villain unties her and drags her limp body off the tracks, and fucks her. He fucks her even as the train roars by like madness. He takes her with such vulturine bloodlust that for a moment the past does not exist. There's only the Now. And her white dress in ruins. He upchucks obscenities, gushes fluids, voids rages, floods her womb, marks her psyche, soils, begrimes everything that could be said to BE her. Until she's done to the brim. Full. And he's empty. And then he's finished. His clutch loosens, his eyes glaze, his body becomes indifferent. He stands, pulls up his pants, wipes himself off on the tail of his shirt, and starts walking home. As if you'd never existed. You look after him. You make your way to your feet. And. You. Follow him. And here we are. You and me. In reality. I tell you this tale. You can't speak. Your legs are spread. You listen to this story of the girl on the train tracks. And so many things pass through your mind to say to me, some scornful, some pleading, some accommodating. But you are enjoined through circumstance to remain silent. Your inner journey's mysterious conclusion unknown even to you. Because a process endured without benefit of civilized response leads to an outcome beyond the imagination of thought.

EVOLUTION
Jonathan Marc Sherman

Comic
Henry, twenties

Henry is talking to his dad about the thesis he is writing on Charles Darwin.

HENRY: I'm writing my thesis without using the letter *e*. . . .
It's a *challenge*. I can't *use* "challenge," though. Can't use "use" . . .
It's *rough*. But *obstacles* — can't use "obstacles." Can't use "impedi-
ments" . . . or "hurdles" . . . *things that block your way* push you to
fulfilling places . . . can't use "places," but you get the point. I don't
use "evolution" . . . or "survival of the *fittest*" . . . or *"descend* . . . with
modifications." Omission of the letter *e* is my cardinal rule. Otherwise, I'm free to go wherever my mind and my research take me. I'm
telling you, the voluntary subtraction of the most popular vowel from
our twenty-six letter alphabet has already been liberating. It's kind
of the fulfillment of a boyhood dream of mine. For my twelfth birth-
day, my father gave me two books written entirely without using the
letter *e* . . .
. . . George Perec wrote *La Disparition* without using a single
e, albeit in *French*. Gilbert Adair did the translation, also without a
single *e*, which goes by the title *A Void*. And an American novel called
Gadsby had a totally *e*-less text, but its dust jacket advertised it as a
book written entirely without the letter *e*. I'm going to use the ini-
tial *H* instead of my first name to avoid even having an *e* on my
dust jacket. (Beat.) There are precedents. They inspire me to continue my work.

EVOLUTION
Jonathan Marc Sherman

Comic
Henry, twenties

> *Henry started this play planning to write a dissertation on Charles Darwin, but through an amusing sequence of events he is now a TV producer, interviewing a man who wants to write for his show.*

HENRY: *(Beat.)* I should tell you some of my cardinal rules and pet peeves before we go any further. My list of "Don'ts," as it were. *(Beat.)* You might want to write this down. . . .

   (Machine-gun quick.) No use of any of the following expressions: "to tell the truth"; "death and taxes"; "love and war"; "at least you've got your health." No jokes about mother-in-laws, or mothers-in-law, or blind dates, computer dates, or constipation. No love triangles, cops and robbers, or flies in soup. Nothing about sleeping on the wet spot. Nothing about not putting the cap back on the toothpaste or pickle-eating pregnant women or hookers with hearts of gold or not being able to program the VCR. No montages or parodies of other TV shows or movies where our characters play *their* characters. No references to the fact that Evian is *naive* spelled backwards. Nothing about big dicks, big tits, or fat people. You can't use any word that has the letter *e* in it — *just kidding.* And absolutely nothing vaguely or bluntly referring to *flatulence. No fart jokes.* They turn my stomach. I don't care if everybody does it. Not on my show. Is that clear? . . . What's the sickest fantasy you've ever had? . . .

   First thing that comes into your brain. . . .

   Interesting. *Very* interesting . . . *(Beat.)* Your sample script shows promise, *Rex.* Welcome aboard.

FEED THE HOLE
Michael Stock

Comic
John, twenties

John is on the phone talking to his friend, Chris.

JOHN: This is the worst day ever, Chris. I'm Depressed Chopra . . . Don't worry, honey, I'm not going to redecorate the apartment again. Well, it's just no fun to do it alone . . . No, I gave up on the Atkins; I started the Ramadan diet. Because I've never met a fat Muslim. So I'm fasting sunrise to sunset and then all the ice cream I want. I figure I can blow up in time to be a Macy's Day float . . . Well, I'm just freaking out. Aren't you freaking out? I'm in the checkout, I can't tell the difference between the *National Enquirer* and the *New York Times* . . . The headlines are the same! Scaring us into some apocalyptic mindset. Well, sure, Chris, they may have nuclear capabilities, but we don't know. And why? Because they won't tell us. We have a history of being lied to . . . How can being lied to be for your own good? . . . No, not because we're Americans. They hate us because we show 'em we care, make promises to be there, and then leave 'em when they need us most. I'm not insinuating anything. Chris, I'm talking about the U.S. government, not about how you leave me. I'm telling you. Our streets will continue to run with blood . . . No, not nukes. We should be scared of the disenfranchised; who are so hurt, so unsatisfied, they see no other way but to lash out . . . Well, this thing with Shelly's got me thinking. She's just acting out to make herself happy and — No, I'm not happy with you gone, I'm not happy with — Oh, hold on. *(Clicks over to call waiting.)* Hello? Oh, hey Rob . . . No, she's running late. Great! See ya soon. Bye, babe. *(Assuming an overtly straight voice.)* I mean, later, doggie-dog, dude. *(Clicks back to Chris.)* Sorry. It was Rob . . . He's fine. Yes, totally, he's fine, he just keeps shitting everywhere. Of course I tell him "Don't shit in the house." . . . No, I don't think he confuses "sit" and "shit." You really think he doesn't understand "SIT, I'll give you a treat, you good dog, I love you" and "Don't SHIT on my Pradas you fucking asshole"?! . . . I'm this close to turning him into a fucking throw pillow, so help me God . . . It's like, "I give you un-whatever it is — unquestioned love, un —" . . . huh? Right, no, right, unconditional love — hah, my therapist would get a kick out of that, I couldn't remember "unconditional love," how apropos. Anyway, "I give you unconditional love and feed you brown pebbles, so if you wanna shit in the house, grow opposable thumbs, get a job, rent an apartment, and shit all over it." It was your idea to get this dog, and then you leave me here to pick up its shit! . . . Well, he does — even when I yell the hell out of him, that sighing squeal he makes is satiated joy. I think he's acting out. Shitting as a cry for help . . . Because he misses you — and, maybe he's afraid he'll get nuked.

A FEW STOUT INDIVIDUALS

John Guare

Dramatic
Harrison, forties

> *Harrison, a former Union soldier, is talking about the terrible carnage at the battle of Cold Harbor. He is talking to Ulysses S. Grant and Samuel L. Clemens.*

HARRISON: Charge! The bodies fall. We can't get out on the field to clear the wounded, much less the dead. Thousands of men dying. Charge! Charge! The men fall. A mountain of flesh. The shooting won't stop. Who's running this battle? Ulysses S. Grant. Unconditional Surrender Grant. Men climb up the wall of bodies. Charge! Grant is wasting his men. We are killing our own men — . . .

I pick up a white flag and run up that mountain. Cease fire! In the name of everything good, cease fire! Me at Cold Harbor waving that flag. That's as close to God as I ever came. Or as close as God ever came to me. . . .

I only waved my flag for a few moments. I was shot. In India they put their dead in the rivers. I didn't have to go to India to see that! There was darkness. There must have been a cease-fire because the nurses and soldiers who lived threw us thousands of corpses into wagons to take us and burn us . . . Well, one of those corpses came to and crawled out from under a stack of corpses — a corpse called me. My eyes and ears and nose opened all at once and I thought I was in a butcher's abattoir from the stink of flesh, the taste of blood, not my blood, but other people's blood that had seeped into my mouth. I feel the weight of the flesh, corpses twitch in rigor mortis over me, under me. I hear the groaning of the dead all over me, beside me. I thought dead would be quiet but we were bumping over stones on the way to the fire. Air moving out of corpses. I moved my fingers. I was not dead. The man over me. Under me. The right of me. The left of me. They were dead. Was I one of them? How had I stayed alive? I must have eaten the flesh around me. Drunk the blood around me for water. I can smell smoke. Flesh. They were burning corpses. They had to. Not enough earth to bury all this dead. Scoop up all the sand in the Sahara, collect all the dirt of the Steppes of Russia — not enough earth to cover all these Cold Harbor dead. But I am not one of them! Don't put me in the fire! I pushed my way up through the weight of stinking flesh. Was dying like being born? My hand reached out of the dead wagon and grabbed a soldier by the arm. He saw my eyes open and screamed loud — Stop the wagon! The moving wagon stopped. Don't put me in fire. Not fire! I am not dead. I swear. Soldiers prodded me with a bayonet. Do you think the black one's telling the truth? My lips moved. I'm telling the truth. They pulled me out of the flesh the way you'd rescue a drowning swimmer out of the sea. How many more alive men were in those wagons headed to the flames? We have to live for them. Are we still in that death wagon struggling to get out from under that ton of corpses?

FISHER KING

Don Nigro

Dramatic
Major John Pendragon, fifty-four

> *Major John Pendragon, a Union Officer in the Civil War, has got-*
> *ten separated from the rest of the Army while on a reconnaissance*
> *mission with some soldiers from his Ohio Volunteers, he and is now*
> *lost in the middle of nowhere, in the wilderness where Maryland,*
> *Virginia, West Virginia, and Pennsylvania come together. The sol-*
> *dier who's supposed to be his scout — a big, childlike, rather sim-*
> *ple-minded young man named Rudd Rhys — has gotten them*
> *hopelessly lost, then realized that he's not far from the carnival tent*
> *of his own father and sister. Rudd has convinced the Major to stop*
> *a minute to check on Rudd's family, but now, when it's time to go,*
> *Rudd doesn't want to leave. The Major is a good man and a good*
> *soldier who hates war and is trying to keep his people alive, one of*
> *whom is his son, Gavin. He knows that if Rudd directly disobeys an*
> *order on the field of battle he's to be shot, and he can't let him get*
> *away with this in front of the rest of his men, and he very much*
> *does not want to shoot him. But he will if he has to.*

PENDRAGON: We can't stay, Rudd. We got to get to camp before night.
These woods are still full of Rebs. I let you come by this way to check
on your folks a minute, and now you've seen them, and they're fine,
and we've got to keep going. If you cause me any more trouble today,
it'll be the last time. Gunfire on the other side of them hills. We gotta
go. Gavin, if that stupid bastard doesn't get up and come along with
us, shoot him. You got that? If he sits there thirty seconds after I walk
away from here, you shoot him. And if you don't shoot him, I'll come
back here and shoot him myself. I'm tired of fooling around with a
bunch of Goddamned children. There's a whole mess of folks wearin
gray uniforms out in them woods, Rudd, and I don't want to alarm

you, but I think they're trying to kill us. I hate this war, I hate the Army, I hate being an officer and I hate stupid people, and you, Rudd, are the stupidest damned son of a bitch I ever met in my life, not to mention the worst Goddamned scout in the history of geography. There's people I miss, too, Rudd. You join the Army and you make an agreement. You follow orders like everybody else. You had time to visit your family before this, but you were too busy drinking and whoring around, and now you think it's my fault because keeping you jackasses alive is more important to me than eating chicken with somebody's sister. Does that make sense to anybody but you?

FIVE FLIGHTS
Adam Bock

Comic
Tom, twenties to thirties

Tom is a professional hockey player. He's also a gay guy who loves ballet.

TOM: I love the ballet. I mean. The ballet. . . . Of course. Oh yeah of course. I'll go and see it a couple of times. I love the ballet. Man I. I'm a hockey player you know so I love it, it's the same in a way, the movement, it's the same, I mean you take Russian nineteenth-century ballet, it's just like a hockey game, it's got five acts, Russian ballet — five acts, act one, narrative it's the story told from beginning to end, act two's a vision, act three is mad scenes, act four the conclusion, act five, a frivolous dance. Now hockey — the game is like the first act of the ballet when the story is told, it's the narrative, the hockey game itself. Then the second act, that's the moment of when it's over, in your mind's eye there's that moment, that critical goal, that incredible, amazing save, or the penalty, that something that was the defining moment that brought us here, it's like act two in the ballet, that moment is a vision. Act three, we won euphoria, or act three, we lost despair, madness, act four, the interviews, the commentary, the coaches' recap, it's all over it's all wrapped up this is what happened this and this and then act five I have to go dance because I'm so fired up I couldn't go to bed. I gotta go dance. I gotta keep moving. I love the ballet.

FIVE FLIGHTS
Adam Bock

Dramatic
Andre, twenties to thirties

> *Andre, a pro hockey player, is talking to another player in the locker room.*

ANDRE: I was down near the bus station today. . . . So I saw this little kid, little you know, maybe three maybe four. With his mom and his grandma, they're all waiting for the bus, this little kid's looking up into the sky, his chin's up like this, he's screaming his head off in Spanish he's yelling and laughing yelling more and laughing, his mom and his grandma are laughing and smiling at the rest of us, I'm thinking How come they're not telling him to shut up and be polite you know because he is screaming. A lot. And loud. So I look at the mother, she smiles at me and looks a little embarrassed because she should be, but she says to me, we can't stop him because he's praying. He's shouting up to God.

 The kid's a total fucking hot shit. He knows already that as long as he's shouting up to God, he can be as noisy as he wants. There's his grandma laughing at him screaming! Hey God hey God hey God hey God in Spanish!

 I was laughing and I got upset. . . .

 I got upset because my kid he's going to be a hot shit like that little kid. I know it. . . .

 I got upset because what if I'm not good enough to him? *(Pause.)* . . .

 You know?

FIVE FLIGHTS

Adam Bock

Seriocomic
Tom, twenties to thirties

> *Tom, a pro hockey player and a gay guy, is talking to Ed, for whom he has fallen.*

TOM: I know you're not going to. I got that. I understand. I got that. But I like you. And even if.

I like you so . . .

It's just I. I love hockey. I love the ballet. It's. I love. Because of the movement. That's what it. Because when I move. I go back into my body. That's why I love hockey. It's why I love the gym. Same reason why I dance. Or when I have sex. Or.

Cause I come back to myself.

(Long pause.)

Like six months ago before I met you I went to a sex club for the first time. Right?

(Smiles.)

You know? You ever been? And I and I remember thinking so why, I mean, I don't need, but for some reason I really wanted I mean I wanted to see it, I wanted to find out what it was like. So I went, over on Otis Street, paid my ten bucks, up the stairs, and it's two floors there, with men all different kinds of men, wandering around a maze, looking. It was like poetry or No it was like dance too, the men walk by each other sort of a little slow, silent, in this dim sort of, might murmur and might might trail a hand across my stomach to tell me that.

And I remember I remember I remember smiling cause I'd found another way to get back into. I found another place I could move.

I think rejection, rejection can be so strong, sometimes, from out there, I mean yeah, or from in here, or from other guys, or from them

It's like the rejection bounces us out of our bodies. It bounces us out of our bodies. Right. And we have to find a way back in.

And I'm going to do anything, I'm going to, I'm

Cause that's. No.

What I can hear, what I hear from you, you don't want to be here. Something, or more than, and you. Right? You don't I hear that.

But I also. I also.

I just wanted to say to you, it's not OK to just give up.

FOR REASONS THAT REMAIN UNCLEAR
Mort Crowley

Dramatic
Patrick, forties

*Patrick, on holiday with an elderly priest, here confronts the man,
who may or may not have sexually abused him years ago.*

PATRICK: *(Icily.)* You look a bit green around the gills. As green as that
Genepy you've been lapping up. *(Calmly.)* I remember a day, a day
of dread and anxiety the likes of which I have never known again —
although at nine years of age I didn't know what the unnamed thing
in me was. I wonder if you remember that day? . . .

(Without affect.) A cold day one winter when you were colder
than the day outside. I knew something was wrong the moment I
saw your face that morning. The moment you looked away from me
and never looked at me again. I thought I had done something. I
thought something was *my* fault. I couldn't eat at the lunchtime recess — the smell of sausage in the cafeteria made me ill. I couldn't
play in the playground. I couldn't even see clearly, even though there
wasn't any bright sunlight — just a canopy of gray, that chilly, dull
noon. All I could do was wonder and worry and wait for the bell to
come back to class . . . when you finally spoke to me. Without looking at me you told me to stay after school — that you had something
to talk to me about. What had I done? What had I caused to make
you so cold? . . .

The hours dragged by like days that day of dread until, at last,
at three o'clock on that cold, dreadful afternoon, the school bell rang
again and the rest of the students left, leaving me alone with you. And
you locked the door. . . .

You remember there was a mesh grating over the windows in that
room — . . .

And I remember how that day the mesh seemed like a cage to me. The moment you started talking, I wanted to get out of that room. I was going to suffocate. I asked you to unlock the door, and you said, "No, I have to talk to you." *(Patrick crosses to bed platform, stands over Conrad and addresses him directly. Conrad avoids Patrick's gaze.)* You didn't sit beside me at my desk this time — you sat on the one in front of me — you didn't touch me, you kept your distance. You couldn't look at me when you finally said, "What we have been doing has to stop. What we have been doing is wrong. What we have been doing is a sin." Do you remember? . . .

You unlocked the door and let me go. And I've never felt free again. After that — the hours, the days left in that year — the interminable anxiety of having to be near you in the classroom, hearing your voice day after day. Seeing you in the schoolyard at recess, playing with the other children — running into you on the stairs, in the corridors, never having our eyes meet again, never knowing what was going on in your mind. Then, coming back after the summer and suddenly finding out you were gone. Disappeared. They said you'd been transferred. I never knew where, never knew what happened to you, never heard of you again. Until this day.

THE GOOD GERMAN
David Wiltse

Dramatic
Siemi, twenties to thirties

> *Siemi, a German man, is talking to some other Germans about the*
> *appeal of Hitler.*

SIEMI: You've known a few, I suppose? Personally, I mean? . . .

Pleasant enough, weren't they? That's part of the danger, some of them are quite charming. Getting to know them individually is not a good idea. Like having a pet snake. One can grow fond of anything on an individual basis. It's hard to truly hate anyone you actually know in person. . . .

Why are we so afraid to admit to it? It's the most natural emotion of all. Because that's not what good little Christians feel? Because our mothers tell us to be nice? Then why do we have it in us? Why is it always so close to the surface, waiting to explode? The Russians were our friends a matter of months ago, now they're subhuman beasts and we hate them and we are happy to hate them. We enjoy hating them. . . .

We revel in it. We love to hate. It is so liberating to be given permission, to be encouraged to indulge the most intense of our passions. That's Hitler's genius, that's what that egomaniacal little runt understood instinctively, it feels good to hate. What other emotion makes you feel so alive? Can one feel one's blood bubbling and skin prickling whenever the Turks are mentioned because one loves the whole swarthy bunch of them? No. But can just the mention of their name set your heart pounding if you hate them? How long can you feel joy? A minute, two? Happiness, whatever that is? Once a month, once a year? Even lust goes away, but you can hate all day, all year, you can hate for a lifetime. It's the one reliable, lasting passion in the human makeup. You can feel the same intense arousal, the pressure in your head, the racing of your heart, the churning in your stomach any time, every time, all the time. . . .

It's genius, Karl. How else could such a man become the leader of the most intelligent nation in the world? We were adrift, we weren't certain who we were anymore, our history alone was not enough so he told us who we were by telling us who we were not. We are Those who are not Them! . . . He circumvented our intelligence, he ignored our minds and went straight for the heart. . . .

Are you immune? Or is it just the word *hatred* that you object to? Would it sound better with a different name? What if we call it something more acceptable, oh, *patriotism,* for instance? Don't you believe it's wonderful! Try it! Join a few thousand of us, come to a rally, listen to the music, march with your heart in your throat and your guts in your head and your lungs bellowing "Heil Hate! Heil Hate! Heil Hate!"

HOUSE ARREST:
A Search for American Character In and Around the White House, Past and Present
Anna Deavere Smith

Dramatic
George Stephanopoulos, thirties

> *The former assistant to President Clinton tells what it's like to work in the White House.*

"THE DEAL"

Sipping a martini.

GEORGE STEPHANOPOULOS: We're a celebrity culture,
   and the president is the Celebrity-in-Chief.
   I think the only private time a president has,
   is when he's in the Oval —
   and he walks from the Oval
   to either his private study or his private bathroom.
   That's it!
   Once he's in the residence he can move *between* rooms
   But there's still some servants around.
   As far as officially, the only truly private time he has is within that small suite,
   which is one
   (He counts.)
   It's four rooms, plus a terrace and one of those rooms is a bathroom.
   He's sitting at a desk with one of the best views in Washington —
   certainly the best morning light I've ever seen in my life —
   But it's got glass this thick,

that can't be
touched.
You've got a
two secretaries on the outside,
and two Secret Service people between them —
as you move *across* the hall *in* the Oval
there's another room to where,
there's a tiny little pantry and there's another Secret Service agent
there —
And then you get to *my* office
And-every-door —
is wired!
Like if I
moved in the back door,
between my office and the Oval
the Secret Service would know! Because it was wired!
And —
I've never thought of it this way before —
What happens, when you juxtapose incredible, immense, power —
but the price —
I mean it's a different
Um,
It's a different devil's choice!
The price is,
Transparency.
Everything you do is known.
You can be the most *powerful* person in the world *(Upward inflec-
tion.)*
You're going to uh,
have every privilege known to man!
Every whim is going to be catered to!
the deal is —
You can do whatever you want.
The price is that everybody is going to know
everything you do.

JUMP/CUT
Neena Beber

Seriocomic
Dave, teens

> *Dave is worried about where his life is heading, and he is confessing his concerns to his friend, Paul.*

DAVE: I just had a scientific breakthrough, Paulie. Some things are in fast motion and some things are in slow motion and therefore most of life, most of life, 'cause it's on a different speed setting than we have, is just this indistinguishable, undetectable blur. . . .

I'm gonna end up a bum, Paulie. . . .

What if I never get out of the slump. . . .

I just got a glimpse, a glimpse of the future, life after high school, and I am such a fucking bum, man. Someday, someday when everyone is putting on their three-piece suits and ties, including you, Dude, and driving to their big-shot jobs in their big ol' Buicks and shaking hands and smoking cigars and winning, like, Good Citizen Awards from the Rotary Club and driving their kids to Little League and whatever shit, I'll still be sitting on some couch somewhere, except the couch'll be really ratty and smell like cat piss, probably in some five-bucks-an-hour motel, and you'll have forgotten about me except to think once in awhile "Poor David Hummer, have you heard what a sorry bum the guy turned out to be?" . . .

Don't leave me behind, Paulie. . . .

Don't leave me to the Goddamn werewolves. Don't let me die a sorry-ass bum in a stinking hotel room. . . .

I'm not joking, Paulie. You gotta keep me off the ratty couch. Promise. Promise me. You gotta promise me.

JUMP/CUT
Neena Beber

Seriocomic
Dave, teens

Dave is obsessed with a video project he's doing.

DAVE: I need this on film, Paul. What, are you afraid I'm writing "All work and no play makes Dave a dull boy" a hundred times over? Trust me, it's brilliant. . . .

I don't know if I'm ready to blow your mind. Everywhere you look, there's poetry, there's magic, poof, bunny from the hat, mad hatter, hat on a bunny, turn on the camera and call action and catch the action I am in. Is this not brilliance? As in shine, as in sparkle, as in see yourself in reflected glory that's the story, is it not? . . .

. . . I'm better than OK. I'm bursting, K. The world, the world is full of music but it's in your head and you have to listen at night because during the day the sounds will drown you out, people drown, more children drown in swimming pools than by gunfire did you know that? But then why should any child die by gunfire that's what I say, one is too many that's what I say, people need to swim more, turn off that fucking camera, will you? . . .

Soul sapper. That's what that machine is. Sacrilege — that's what's going on here. Creating images as if you are God, creating false gods, you are not God. . . .

Turn that off. Turn that off, the second commandment commands you not, no graven images no images in the image of God and I am that image I am a divine being turn that off, you call yourself a Jew, you, you hypocrite. St. David, that's who I am, a martyr to your sins and this is my feast day, my fucking feast day, and I was thinking about the movie and the movie is the future, the movie is my past when I am in the future and no one's thinking about the future because it comes too fast, it's always on the way and before you know it it's tomorrow and tomorrow and tomorrow creeping in its petty pace but I don't think it's so petty as it turns out, I think it's fucking fast and furious and it doesn't creep, it careens, it cruises, it crashes into Schiller and Schelling and Schopenhauer and suddenly — . . .

— suddenly it becomes clear that they didn't live before us, they live after us on a loop, an infinite loop and all our yesterdays have lighted fools the way to dusty death and all our tomorrows cast a long dark shadow over our todays, that's what I think, Mr. William Shakespeare, if you catch my drift.

KIMBERLY AKIMBO
David Lindsay-Abaire

Comic
Buddy, midthirties

Buddy's wife has been recording thoughts on her current pregnancy. Here Buddy is on the tape recorder. He's somewhere outside. It's snowing.

BUDDY: And the thing is, I don't think I'm very good with kids. I mean I *like* kids, I just never pictured myself as a father. I'm more of a bachelor-uncle type, you know? Which isn't to say I regret anything. I love Kim, and I'm happy you're coming but . . . when you're young you imagine doin' a bunch of different things. Just . . . crazy, unrealistic stuff but . . . And then when Pattie got pregnant with Kim, it was like, "Oh, OK, I guess I do *this* then." Which was fine. Made things easier in some ways, you know, to not have any . . . choices I guess. I mean, most guys in the world are just guys who go to work, right? Guys with kids. So there's no shame in that. Just being a regular person. *(Beat.)* Although I would still like to travel someday. That's something I'd like to do. I'll see these countries on TV and think, "Wow, that's a weird place. I'd like to see that in person maybe." Like Pamplona. That's in Spain, and the bulls run through the streets chasing everybody, and the guys scramble up the sides of buildings and jump in doorways and some people get gored. It looks fun. I'd like that. But you need money to see things, so . . . *(Pause.)* Your mom and I spent a few days on the Jersey Shore once. Right after we got married. Well not *right* after, but when we saved enough. That was nice. And you know what's funny? When we decided to leave Secaucus, I was like, "Alright, we're finally going somewhere." But then we came to Bogota. Which isn't really the someplace I had in mind but . . . What are ya gonna do? *(Beat.)* Those Alamo raffle tickets didn't work out either. It was in the paper. Some retired gardener won. Like *he* needed a vacation. *(Beat.)* See the world, Carmelita. That's my advice to you. *(Beat.)* Pattie's gonna be mad I'm using her tape recorder but . . . I got nothin' else to do. Haven't had a drink in eight days. I promised Kim. See that? I'm a good guy. I don't know what Pattie's been saying on these things, but I'm tellin' you straight. I'm a good guy.

LEAVING TANGIER
David Johnston

Seriocomic
Tap, late teens

*Tap is attending the funeral of a writer whose work he admires very
much. He has met a man who knew the deceased.*

TAP: Tell me everything about him. I want to know everything. . . .

   His books are amazing. There's that description of the desert and
the Bedouins in *Lunch With Cannibals* and then it turns into this
whole Arab warrior thing in the seventh century during the Crusades.
All that stuff linking cannibalism and communion and um um . . .

   . . . Those warriors and sex. I mean, that's intense stuff. I never
got stuff like that in high school. They wanted us to read freaking
Silas Marner. Freaking *Song of Hiawatha* bullshit. Oswin was cool.
You know what I loved about him, Mr. Cooper? . . .

   What I loved about him. Why I wish I'd met him. Was when
he tore up the maps. . . .

   When he tore up the maps. That part in *Peyote Nights* when
they're in the jungle and they tear up their maps 'cause they've decided they're going to find their own way out and they know they
might die but they do it anyway. That was him. That's what he did.
With his own life. I mean, everything is mapped out here. Your whole
life. Know what I mean? . . .

   Me and Rosemund, we live in Grandmom's house — where
Uncle Oswin lived when he was a kid. Daddy died when we were
kids and Momma died of breast cancer five years ago and we check
in on Grandmom at the home. And I finished high school and Rosemund says, OK, Tap, it's the Army or a job, there's no money for college. So I went to work for the Wal-Mart and I became assistant
manager of the hardware department and now I'm up for assistant
store manager and that training takes eleven weeks and everyone is

happy 'cause I'm advancing in the organization and everyone at work is nice all the time, 'cause — you know — it's Wal-Mart. And I'll get married in a coupla years, 'cause — you know — you get married. And I'll have kids and buy a little house in Powhatan and get fat and work at Wal-Mart and the car'll break down all the time and Rosemund'll hate my wife no matter who she is, she's just gonna hate her and my kids won't talk to me and I'll look at the TV and maybe my wife'll leave me and I'll start drinking late at night by myself in the garage, drinking bourbon out of little Styrofoam cups late at night in the garage and then I'll fall down and need a new hip or get senile and go into the home or just die. *(Pause.)* I'm sorry, Mr. Cooper, what was your question?

A LETTER FROM ETHEL KENNEDY

Christopher Gorman

Dramatic
Kit, late twenties

Kit, a TV executive who is HIV-positive, is talking to his father over lunch.

KIT: It's that Christmas Eve the cops brought you home at two in the morning. Jimmy and I saw the cop car with you in the beard and red suit and thought they were arresting Santa Claus. . . .

I watched this whole scene from the staircase. Mom was wearing that terry-cloth robe with stop and go signs for buttons. She screamed she was going to divorce you, which for some crazy reason, terrified me back then. You got up and staggered into the hallway, knocking pictures off the walls. Mom pushed you into your bedroom. There was a lot of yelling, then nothing. I could hear the oven clock ticking. Mom came back down the hall. She unplugged the Christmas tree lights and dragged the tree — it was a big one that year — ornaments were smashing, light bulbs were breaking. I stuck my head through the banister and saw her drag it into your room. "Merry Christmas, shithead!" I believe she dragged the tree on top of you in bed. Then the door slammed and Mom went into the kitchen and sat at the table, smoking cigarettes. I fell asleep on the stairs. The next morning the tree was back in the living room — Barbie dolls and Lionel trains . . . like nothing had happened.

THE LOVE SONG OF J. ROBERT OPPENHEIMER

Carson Kreitzer

Dramatic
Oppie, midforties

> *J. Robert Oppenheimer here is forty-five years old. This monologue,
> a memory of his first love, who committed suicide soon after their
> last meeting, takes place during his appearance before a committee
> investigating his communist contacts. This committee will revoke his
> security clearance, leaving him unable to participate in cutting-edge
> nuclear science for the remainder of his life.*

OPPIE: Surveilled and surveilled and surveilled.
    Wartime and beyond.
    WHAT IS THIS, RUSSIA?

    The last night I spent with a woman who felt Death breathing down
        her back.
    That last night Violated. As they watched the house. Or had it
        Bugged.
    Our last sad . . . love.
    There were tears involved, if I recall correctly. all these years later.

    I recall correctly.
    I recall . . . everything.
    Blue veins across her white skin.
    Freckles on her shoulders from the sun.
    The curve of her back as she . . . bent to unbuckle a shoe.
    Those eyes.
    That I had . . . got lost in. Many a time.
    Now *she* was lost in them.
    Staring out of her face at me, as if

as if I possessed some sort of Answer and when I didn't . . .

I, who was now no longer lost in the unswimmable green depths of
    her eyes but
Found
in the yellow sand of Los Alamos.

I saw her there, receding from the world.
like a ghost
But I was of the world now, in the world and I had to serve it. To
    save it. Not her.
Anymore.

Just this one night to hold her thin shaking body in my arms.
As security men waked and watched from their cars outside.

The tears that night were hers.
I held mine until the news of her death, some weeks later.
I left my desk and went to stand alone among the tall pines.
They were not the same green as her eyes.
Nothing was.
But they were green. And smelled sweet.
And made a little mournful rustling for me. In accompaniment to
    my ridiculous silent rictus of weeping. Alone on a ridge in New
    Mexico.

No, the security men must not have bugged the house.
Or they would know
We did not speak of Communism that night.

MY OLD LADY
Israel Horovitz

Dramatic
Matthias, forties

> *Matthias, an American man, has inherited an apartment in Paris,*
> *inhabited by an elderly woman who, he has learned, has the legal*
> *right to live there until she dies, and who also had a long romance*
> *with his father.*

MATTHIAS: Sorry, Madame Giffard, but, I'm not seeing the wonder of you
in the slightest. You've found some sort of justification for what you
did to me and my family in the name of love! *Give it up!* You're not
getting off the hook! What you did did me in! And you don't even
know how to fucking say "I'm sorry"! No wonder he loved you! You're
his soul mate! My father never said "I'm sorry" to anyone in his en-
tire *life!* . . .
   . . . Max Gold was the least grateful, coldest son of a bitch I have
ever known, and I've known some *très froide.* . . .
   Wait a minute, wait a minute, wait a minute! You'll hear it, if I
want to say it! I've just spent a couple of hours with you telling me
that my father was some kind of Casanova and Saint John the Divine,
combined, and I'm supposed to listen and nod, understandingly . . .
but, when I try to point out that, as fathers go, my father, in his rela-
tionship with his wife and children, was a little less like St. John and a
little more like Captain Hook, you *"simply won't hear it"!?* . . .
   . . . Look, Mrs. Giffard . . . you're an old lady. You've got ninety-
two to ninety-four years behind you. All real-estate considerations
aside, you could have a good couple of years ahead of you as well.
Whatever my father was to you, he was . . . *to you.* I believe you. I
don't doubt for a second that you're telling the truth. But, that particular truth is *your* truth, not mine . . . and, certainly, not hers . . .
not my mother's. *(Beat.)* This is *crazy! (And then . . .)* I don't have a

friend in the world, Madame Giffard. Not one. I owe money, every-where. When people I used to know — former friends — if they see me coming, they cross the street! They know I've got this loser-virus, and if they come too close, they're liable to catch it. . . .

. . . I drink too much. I have no confidence, no courage, no *vision!* Don't people like you and my father ever wonder *why? (He pours and drinks a full glass of whiskey.)* Do you think self-esteem is some kind of a *birthright?* Do you think self-esteem is some kind of, I dunno, *natural phenomenon,* like a physical fact? The baby's born; the doctor slaps his little ass and says "He's OK! He's got all his fingers and toes, he's got a little dick, he's got his self-esteem. He's OK." *(Beat.)* It doesn't work that way, lady. If you wanna kill a kid, you don't shoot him! You just do *nothing!* You just withhold your love, and watch the child wither and devote his miserable loveless life to pleasing you. To *displeasing* you! At some point, the child says "I've got to stop try-ing!" *BUT, YOU CAN'T STOP TRYING!* You think everybody else in the world is loved, but not you. You've got this terrible secret that eats you alive! You think you're . . . *WHY AM I TELLING YOU THIS? . . . WHY DO I CARE? . . .* I cannot imagine that my parents spent a lot of time trying to organize my birth. I can only imagine my mother, des-perately unhappy, sobbing in the night. And my father, home from travel, from your bed, throwing in a midnight mercy fuck. Then, she's pregnant with me, with this endless reminder of blah-blah-blah . . .

MY SWEETHEART'S THE MAN IN THE MOON

Don Nigro

Comic
Harry, early thirties

> *In New York, in 1902, Mr. Harry K. Thaw, the demented Pittsburgh millionaire, age thirty-one, has become deeply infatuated with a beautiful young chorus girl named Evelyn Nesbit. In this early scene, Harry has come to make a formal call on Evelyn, and he is sitting in the parlor with her and her mother. Harry sits on a wooden chair, fumbling with his hat, which is on his knees, and trying to make small talk, which he is not good at. Harry is intelligent, not without charm, and has a rather engaging sense of humor, but his mind tends to jump around like a box full of rabbits. He is doing his best to make polite conversation, since he wants desperately to make a good impression, but Mrs. Nesbit is rather suspicious of him, and she has just asked him, as politely as she could, what exactly he's doing there.*

HARRY: Good question. Fair enough. Let's just reach right
　　down into the rabbit's chest cavity, and pull
　　the beating heart out, as it were. I've come
　　to pay a call, not frivolously, although
　　I am, I must admit, perhaps as acquainted
　　with frivolity as the next man is, depending of course
　　on who the next man is, because I'm a great
　　admirer of your daughter's work. I mean
　　her modeling work, and her work in the theater, if
　　you call that work, and I know some do, but I've
　　become concerned that your daughter, being a virgin,
　　is far too innocent for the stage, which is
　　as any God-fearing American citizen knows,

the Devil's clog dancing academy. This girl
should be in school. This girl should be in knee socks,
and one of those little plaid skirts. And her brother — if
indeed she has a brother — should be in school
as well, although I wouldn't expect him to wear
the little plaid skirt, except in Scotland, of course,
where it doesn't matter, because they drink a lot
of Scotch there, and the women have red hair
and a kind of windblown, freckly, wet-mouthed beauty,
and bad teeth, but I'd be proud and gratified
to put your children somewhere near Woonsocket,
where there is excellent fox hunting, to rescue
your daughter from that satanic monstrosity
which passes for the American theater.

THE NOTEBOOK

Wendy Kesselman

Comic
Warren, thirteen

*In this direct address to the audience, Warren confides in us his love
of books and his fear of an imperious teacher.*

WARREN: *(Light comes up on Warren Stone, thirteen, sitting on the edge of
the stage, busy writing in a small red notebook. The light suddenly ex-
posing him, he looks up anxiously, then leans forward, speaks to us con-
fidentially.)* I have a secret. A terrible secret. No one knows. No one
in the world. Except my parents. They have to. They live with me.
But my secret . . . *(In a hushed whisper.)* I like to read. What am I
saying . . . "like." Get up every morning, go to bed every night,
breathe, dream, tremble, *live* to read! I would die without my books.
And my father's books. And my mother's. The things I've read, the
things I've learned in those books of theirs! Books filled with philosophy, psychology, love, sex, murder, *death!* Sometimes I think I should
hide their own books from them. *(A pause.)* I mean, I'll read anything — cereal boxes, graffiti . . . But books! That first moment with
a brand-new untouched book. Running my hand over the sleek shin-
ing cover. Opening it in the silence of my room. That first page. Those
first words. *(Quiet.)* And you know what's even better than a new
book? *(Silence.)* An old one. The worn leather cover, the soft secret
smell! What hands have touched these pages, devoured these words
in some faraway room long long ago? *War and Peace.* My favorite!
Exactly one thousand, four hundred and forty-four pages long. Why
does it have to end? *(His eyes bright.)* I bought it from this amazing
man at a secondhand bookstore on the Lower East Side. And in it I
found the one person I'd waited for my whole life, the person I'd die
for, my favorite, my only heroine — the radiant, divine . . . Natasha!
(A pause.) But I can't go into that now. Because now there's another

story, a story that's burned itself into me as much as any book. And it's all in here — *(Opening the small red notebook.)* in my notebook — every word, every moment, every scene! *(He leans even closer to us.)* You see . . . there's this teacher, this terrible teacher. Almost as terrible as my secret. More terrible perhaps. I've been at Sheffield my whole life, but she's been there forever — it's as if she came with the school, or the school came with her. And the funny thing is, she's not even American. She's English. From England. But it's not just that she's from another country, she's from another time, another century! *(A pause.)* Miss Thorne. *(Light comes up on Miss Thorne at her desk. With electrifying blue eyes, silky white hair, a china doll complexion, she wears an old-fashioned dress and holds a book of poetry.)* Like a thorn in my side, a thorn in my heart. Everyone calls her "Thorny." Not to her face of course — the whole school's in absolute awe of her. Especially the high-school girls. At Sheffield, after eighth grade . . . girls! All girls! They quiver, quake, drop into a dead faint when she calls on them. *(He pauses.)* But Thorny's made the high school famous. And everyone puts up with her because they know she's the best teacher, maybe the only *real* teacher the school has ever had.

OUR LADY OF 121st STREET
Stephen Adly Guirgis

Dramatic
Rooftop, thirties

> *Rooftop is a popular Los Angeles D.J., looking to reconcile with the love of his life.*

ROOFTOP: I'm a make this call 'cuz I have to, but I need you to think on this till I get back: Ain't my fault about your husband, dass on you. And it ain't my fault 'bout your scorched-up heart — you married me juss like I married you. And I got no choice but to try and forgive myself for everything I done to you, 'cuz, what's the fuckin' alternative, Inez? I usta think there was some other option, some way 'round it, but there really ain't. I can try an' forgive myself, or, I can go jump off the GW — and dass it! I feel guilty 'bout a girl been dead fifteen years, and you? You angry at a boy — a boy, Inez — not me . . . Do I wish I had done it different back then? Hell yeah. Even now, I'm tempted to take this conversation in another direction juss so I could get with you. And I could get with you if I worked my game right, don't tell me I couldn't cuz I'm a fuckin' professional — but what would be the point a that? I lost you — dass my cross. 'Cuz you was my royal. And I killed it. But if you wanna walk around all these years later still tryin' ta play dead, dass your waste, not mine . . . dass on you. I'm a make my call now.

PENDRAGON

Don Nigro

Seriocomic
Twain, seventy-five

> *Mark Twain, an old writer, in the year 1910, not long before his death, sits on the front porch of his home in Connecticut drinking with his old friend, journalist John Rhys Pendragon, trying to make sense of his life.*

TWAIN: It was once my hope, as a young man, that God, like a cunning playwright, gives us the opportunity to endure inexplicable and apparently unendurable amounts of grief, disappointment, humiliation, betrayal, agony, sickness, and loss in order that we might appreciate more deeply the joy that awaits us at the end of the play. But then I was, on the whole, a remarkably stupid young man. I don't know when it was that I finally admitted to myself that this is all a bunch of horse flop. I then came up with five or six possible explanations for the state of the world as I found it: One, that God is a pleasant fantasy. Two, that God is indifferent to our suffering, wishing us neither good nor ill — he just doesn't care. Three, that God cared once but has gotten interested in something else and forgotten all about us. Four, that God is mentally unbalanced, and therefore not to be held accountable for his actions. Five, that God is a sadistic, cannibalistic butcher. Six, that God's understanding of what's going on here is as far beyond my limited ability to comprehend the meaning of events as my rather intelligent cat's ability to fathom the *Encheiridion* by Epictetus, and therefore no amount of intellectual circumgyration on my part will ever enable me to understand the isolated death of one young girl, let alone the apparently infinite barbaric and hideous myriads of other unspeakable atrocities taking place every second of every hour of every day and year in the bloody history of this particular insignificant piece of universe. The only view, out of all these, that holds any hope for us, of course, is the last one, but if I was you, I wouldn't bet the farm on it. . . .

Plan on dying. That's a pretty safe bet. Kinda hard to collect your winnings, though. Well. Time for me to shuffle on into the big, dark house. The reports of my death will soon prove, I fear, to have been less exaggerated than they seemed at the time. Night.

PENDRAGON
Don Nigro

Seriocomic
Twain, seventy-five

> *Mark Twain, an old writer, in the year 1910, not long before his death, sits on the front porch of his home in Connecticut drinking with his old friend, journalist John Rhys Pendragon, trying to make sense of his life.*

TWAIN: . . . You look right up there, you can see the comet, when the clouds go. I was born in the year of the comet, and all my life I've believed that I would die in the year of the comet, when the comet came round again. And here it is. So I'd damned well better croak pretty soon, or it'll ruin a beautiful story. Structure is always the hardest thing. Have a cigar. I try to smoke just enough of these damned foul-smelling things to keep me on schedule. My theory was, if I smoke too many, I might die too soon, and spoil the whole thing. But if I didn't smoke enough of them, then I might just live past my time, a fate which, on the whole, I do not recommend. Consult *King Lear*. So now it's nineteen-ten, and the comet is back, and I'm still here, so I've been smoking the damned things like a chimney stack. Sometimes when I'm alone I smoke three or four at the same time. I believe I'm back on schedule, but I can't be certain, of course, until God sees fit to switch me off. You believe in God? . . .

If there is such a creature, lurking out there in the great dark, where the comet lives, I'm not sure I want to know. I'm not certain I want to meet a gentleman who'd create a universe in which one is forced to watch everything one has been idiotic enough to get suckered into conceiving any affection for being systematically tortured and mutilated and ultimately destroyed before one's eyes, or at the very least turning into some revolting caricature of what one used to bring chocolates to on Friday evenings and sit in the parlor with. . . .

No, I don't laugh. I make other jackasses laugh, from time to time — their manner of snarling safely in mobs at the pathetic, hopeless truths I hand them — but I do not laugh, myself. No. Not for a long time. All the laughter died with my wife, it died with my daughter Susy, of spinal meningitis, drowned in the bathtub with my other, epileptic daughter, who once tried to murder the cook. All the laughter has died in me, and there was much to die. I was at one time the biggest jackass of them all. *(Pause. Twain drinks.)* Drink some more. Eventually, you know, the alcohol will blind you. Then you can see better in the great dark where pretty soon the comet goes and I go with it. Take my advice, Rhys. Have no children. Create nothing. It only gives the son of a bitch more ways to get at you. *(Twain finishes his drink.)* Woops. Kidneys. The kidneys of once proud old men — another example of the Lord's bountiful sense of humor. I must go and water the begonias. Waste not, want not. Excuse me.

PRIVATE JOKES, PUBLIC PLACES
Oren Safdie

Dramatic
Erhardt, forties

> *Erhardt is an architect and professor of architecture, on a faculty*
> *panel evaluating a student's thesis project.*

ERHARDT: You don't understand a thing I just said, do you? . . .

(Gently.) That's all right. You know, when I first came to this
country, I barely spoke English and — . . .

I didn't mean it that way. I just mean to sympathize with you;
there's nothing worse than not understanding something that someone else has told you you're supposed to understand. . . . It makes
you feel so small, so stupid, and you're obviously a very sensitive and
intelligent person . . . So that's fine. Architecture isn't about words,
it's about what's in *(Pounding his chest.)* here. It's about taking space
and transforming it into something magical. We are part of a great
tradition, in which man not only has built shelter to protect himself
from the elements, but has also built cathedrals to pray to gods, con-
structed bridges to cross the river — figuratively as well as physically —
and sometimes we have erected buildings for the pure sake of exciting
the imagination, *(To Margaret.)* perhaps even in an effort to impress a
beautiful woman. . . .

Of course . . . But for thousands of years, architects have tried
to reach up to the heavens, in a sense trying to finish the tower of
Babel . . . But we have been denied. Why? It's a question I have spent
half my life thinking about, and I have finally come to the conclusion that we — man — architects — have been speaking in different tongues. Nobody is on the same page . . . But finally we have
reached a stage in history — thanks to Freud and psychoanalysis —
that we no longer need to communicate verbally, not even physically

or visually . . . but psychologically — the only common experience of every human being, besides death, but there's no use in that . . . And by deconstructing our experiences, distilling them down to the very essence of the human subconscious, we will be able to transcend boundaries that have held us back. And so like the scientist who strives to reverse the effects of aging on human life, or the physicist trying to determine the end of the universe, architects must also move beyond the barriers of what we have come to think of as . . . floor . . . wall . . . ceiling . . . even pool. Only then will we be able to complete The Tower and be one with God, using him as an iconoclast symbol of course, rather than anything with religious connotations . . . But, no, Margaret, don't feel for a minute that architecture is about words . . .

QUICK & DIRTY
David Riedy

Comic
Man, twenties to forties

> *A man is talking to a woman who he may or may not be trying to pick up while waiting for the subway train to come.*

MAN: Do you know what I was thinking? While we were looking at each other? . . .

"What if that lovely woman and I fell onto each other with our mouths open and eyes closed and had each other totally and without fear? It could be something sweet, something fun. What's wrong with tenderness?" *(The train comes to a stop and the doors open. During the following, she steps onto the subway and he puts his foot in front of the door, holding it open:)* The way you looked at me makes me think we could care about each other for a few hours which seems much better than dragging it out for months or years in a complicated ritual of trying to convince yourself that the momentary flash of lust or desire, or love — if you want to call it that — that that feeling can last past its natural lifetime of weeks or even seconds. That's the greatest sin two people can commit together. And I realized that there was nothing to stop us, me and you, or "us" — everyone — the whole world, there's no reason why two people can't be totally honest with each other and share feelings sparked by how someone said "peppercorn" or a smile, just a corner-smile, as they look bashfully down at their shoes, or the casual, unintended brush of someone's hand across your ass as they squeeze by in a doorway, or even the unlikely meeting of sympathetic and interested eyes from across a crowded subway platform.

THE REDEEMER
Cybèle May

Dramatic
Stewart, thirty to fifty

> *Stewart, a detective with the Allentown police, and Connie have
> an uneasy truce as they wait for a break in the case. As they spend
> more time together, he begins to open up more. But his attempts to
> reach out to Connie end up being uncomfortable confessions,*

STEWART: I can't go home. I can't sleep there. I keep having this dream.
> *(Pause.)*
> I'm at camp . . . I think I'm a kid. The kids are out in the river
> on a swimming platform. They're yelling for me, waving me out, I'm
> running back and forth along the shore, like a dog does, you know.
> The rocks are slimy and I keep slipping and my mother's made me
> wear these little canvas sneakers because she was afraid of broken glass
> and snapping turtles.
> *(Pause. He tries to remember.)*
> Suddenly I'm swimming out to them. The water is cold, and
> it's over my head and I feel the weeds pulling at my feet . . . The
> current is washing me downstream and the more I kick the more
> my feet get tangled. I panic and I swallow water and I'm kicking and
> my legs are hurting . . . the kids are screaming now.
> *(Pause.)*
> I get to the platform and pull myself up and . . . and . . . I'm
> in the big lodge now. It's this huge room with tall ceilings with ex-
> posed beams. The kids are gone and it's really quiet. There are these
> big birds all over the place, hopping around on the furniture and the
> tables. Kind of like crows, glossy black with red beaks . . . One starts
> pecking at my hand, at first just lightly. I put my hands in my pock-
> ets, but the other birds hop over their claws ticking on the wood.
> *(Pause.)*

They're all pulling and tearing at my pants to get at my hands . . . I pick up the first bird in front of me by the legs and I start swinging him to get the other ones away. The one in my hands, he doesn't seem to want to get away, he's just calmly biting my hands. I slam him against a table and he keeps doing it, I slam him against the wall . . . over and over again until he is limp in my hands and his feathers are wet and sticky. I drop him to the floor.

(Long silence.)

I'm not asking you to tell me what it means.

(Pause.)

I guess I should leave. I'm sorry. I shouldn't have . . . no, I gotta go.

THE REDEEMER
Cybèle May

Dramatic
Stewart, thirty to fifty

> *As the kidnapper plays games with Stewart and Connie, detectives
> with the Allentown police, Stewart is driven to the edge. When he
> returns from a failed attempt to retrieve the boy, Connie confronts
> him with her knowledge of Stewart's past.*

STEWART: It was an accident. *(Pause.)* We were in the car. We were running late. She was supposed to have hemmed the pants of my suit. She hadn't only I didn't know until I put 'em on so I had to keep them up with masking tape. It looked terrible but she kept saying that we were going to be late. So we were in the car and she looked down at me and said I looked ridiculous and she was glad that she had no standards left otherwise she would be humiliated to be seen with me. That's when I started yelling — what did she want from me? She wanted me to lose control, didn't she? And then she started laughing. The faster I drove the funnier I was and the louder she laughed. I couldn't take it, I couldn't take it anymore. We were ugly. I wanted both of us dead. Suddenly, I wanted it all to be over and I turned straight into the oncoming traffic. *(Pause.)* I forgot Tommy was in the back. I forgot my boy was there. He was all dressed up in his little blue suit. If it hadn't been so messed up in the accident he would have been buried in it. He was so quiet, quiet all the time. Shiny black hair, brown eyes. He had freckles from playing soccer all summer with the neighbor kid in the yard. He'd curl up on my lap and put his face against my chest and tap along with my heart. We used to eat cereal for supper when his mother wasn't home. *(Pause.)* I told everyone it was my fault. They'd just hug me and say it would be OK and that I'd stop blaming myself someday. They didn't realize that I had actually done it, it really was my fault.

THE REEVES TALE

Don Nigro

Dramatic
Alen, twenties

> *In rural East Ohio in 1972 John and Alen, both twenty-seven, college grads who are now drifters, are hired hands at the Pendragon house, a huge old falling-apart mansion, where they work for Sim Reeves, who rents the place to farm the land. John and Alen live in very cramped quarters in a couple of rooms of the house with Sim, who's a vulgar, piglike man, his intelligent and attractive, sad wife Abby, Abby's annoying grandfather Pap, and Abby and Sim's beautiful sixteen-year-old daughter Molkin. Alen is trying to convince John to help him seduce Molkin by distracting Abby while Sim is asleep.*

ALEN: You're talkin' to the guy who babysat your damned German shepherd all the time you was in the service. . . .

He missed you. He committed suicide. Who was it got the shit beat out of him when them rednecks jumped you in the bar that time? Huh? I could have pretended I didn't know you, John. Christ, I lost a tooth in that. Who drove you to El Paso to see that girl with the long hair? Who painted half your apartment? Who went to your mother's funeral with you? Who slept in the dorm lobby when you had Diane Roselli there for the weekend? . . .

I got it all planned, like a military operation, just like the Bay of Pigs or something. OK, bad example. Look, we got three beds here, right? Just like the three bears. Now, before Sim hired us, they slept Sim and Abby in the one over on the end, right?

They're disoriented, John, because to make room for us, we got Molkin's old bed on the other end, which you and me share, and she's in the near bed with Abby, and Sim's in the middle with Pap. So once Sim gets to snoring good, and Molkin goes to sleep, what does Abby do? She goes out in the kitchen and smokes a cigarette. Every night. Just like clockwork. So when she goes out for her smoke, you follow her out there and keep her busy for half an hour or so, talk to her or something. Hell, screw her on the table if she'll let you. That asshole Sim is driving her nuts. She could probably use a little something to take her mind off her life. You know, you two being so sensitive and all.

John, that girl ain't been a flower since she was fourteen. She knows what she's doing, believe me. And Abby don't care. What does she care? Come on, take a chance. You might get lucky. This is America, here. This is like the spirit of free enterprise at work, John. You know what I mean? John? Please? . . .

Attaboy, John. I knew you would. You're a good kid, you sucker. I don't deserve you. I really don't. Boy, this is gonna be some night, huh? . . .

You got to let yourself go more, Johnny. Loosen up a little. I mean, when you're dead, you're dead, right? Life is sweet. Smell the roses, taste the wine. Eat a peach.

THE REEVES TALE
Don Nigro

Comic
Pap, sixties to eighties

> *In the autumn of 1972, Pap, an old man, lives in the falling-apart
> Pendragon mansion in east Ohio with his granddaughter and her
> family, who rent a couple of rooms in the place, and two young men
> who board there and work on the farm. While eating his cornflakes
> with them in the morning, he tries to explain to them how base-
> ball is the secret of life.*

PAP: Never trust a man that don't know baseball. The Cleveland Indians
is a lesson in life. Look good in the spring, then die like a dog. Always get rid of the best ones, Calavito, Cash, Minnie Minoso. When
Herb Score got hit in the face with that line drive, killed the whole
town, right there. Herb does the games on the radio now. Don't know
how the hell he stands it, year after year. Remember Dick Donovan?
Pitch a two-hitter and lose seven to three. Pitch a one-hitter and lose
six to nothing. Pitch ten scoreless innings and go out for a pinch hit-
ter who was batting one sixty-two when Donovan himself had the
only two hits the Indians got all day, Frank Funk come in and throw
one pitch and Killebrew hit the damn thing all the way to
Saskatchewan. Submarine Ted Abernathy, one year he was the whole
bullpen, by September Ted's arm looked like a six-foot hot dog.
Lowenstein, there's a life lesson. Only hit two thirty but in the bot-
tom of the ninth, down two runs with two on and two out and a
oh two count, Lowenstein hit the home run for you, little skinny
feller, run like a chicken, play every position on the field, steal home
like it was nothing, dive head first into a brick wall to catch a foul
ball. They'll sell him like a used car. Sudden Sam. Daddy Wags. If
you're good, they find a way to kill you. Learned everything I know
from the Cleveland Indians. Still, got a couple of good kids in the

minors. Bow-legged Polish shortstop, goes and gets the ball real good, throws it twenty feet over the first baseman's head. Got to work on that part of his game. And a big, strong kid, hits the ball real hard, purple hair. Don't know what Ty Cobb would say about purple hair. Couple of pitchers, who knows? Maybe next year. Did somebody fart?

ROUNDING THIRD
Richard Dresser

Comic
Don, thirties to forties

> *Don is the head coach of a Little League team. Here he is address-*
> *ing his team at the first practice of the year.*

DON: Unfortunately, we don't have much time this morning. The Pep Club
has the gym at ten, so I'll keep this brief. First, congratulations! You're
the luckiest kids in town. You're on my team. I can promise you'll
work hard, learn a lot, and have fun. How do we have fun playing
baseball? One word. Winning. Winning is fun. Losing stinks. I hope
that isn't new information. I don't have a lot of rules. The main one
is this. I am in charge, and what I say goes, without any back talk
or eye rolling or wise-guy questions. When I blow my whistle? You
run to me. If you dawdle, no problem, you just don't play the next
game. Get to the ballpark half an hour before game time. "Is twenty-
nine minutes good enough, Coach?" Sorry. "It's my parents' fault I'm
late." Tough.

    Have your parents talk to me and I don't think we'll have any
problems, assuming you remain on the squad. If you ask to play a
particular position — "Coach, can I play shortstop?" — I guarantee
you won't play shortstop for five games. That's it for rules. I keep them
to the minimum and I take them seriously. *(Checks out the team.)* I'm
glad to see most of you are wearing the equipment we suggested. *(Pick-*
ing someone out.) Philip? Philip Bailey? It is Phil, isn't it? Nice going,
remembering to wear the cup. F.Y.I. it's traditionally worn *inside* the
pants. But that's an interesting look, it could catch on. Whoa, you
can make that change later, Phil! *(Beat.)* Now, we all drop fly balls,
miss grounders, make bad throws, that's baseball. Those are called
physical errors, and I will never yell at you over physical errors. What
is it called when we forget how many outs there are or throw to the
wrong base? Anyone? Those are mental errors, and yes, my friends,
you *will* hear me about mental errors.

ROUNDING THIRD
Richard Dresser

Comic
Michael, thirties to forties

> *Michael is the assistant coach of a Little League team. His son is out in right field (Little League Siberia). During a game Michael is coaching, a fly ball is hit to his kid.*

MICHAEL: Dear God, please let him catch the ball. Just this once, let him know what it feels like to have the ball stay in his glove and not go bouncing past so he chases it in a mad terror with everyone screaming and when he finally finds it he has no idea what to do. We've done that. Many times. Let him catch this ball. Let him have this one memory for the rest of his life, that summer afternoon when the ball fell into his glove and stayed there. And let him jog back to the bench smiling in spite of himself, getting pats on the back from his teammates, still clutching the ball that didn't get away. He's never had that and he may never have the chance again. Check your stats, God, he's twelve years old, his first and last year of Little League, no team for my boy next year. So this is it. Now God, if you're really there — and for the purposes of right now, I'm assuming you are — this is a pretty small request. Last year I asked you to let my wife live, and yes, that was a big one and I know you had your reasons for what happened, which I try to respect although I will never understand. But this should be a no-brainer. The bases are loaded, the score is tied, it's the fifth inning, Frankie has already struck out three times plus a ball got past him in right field and went all the way to the fence — a bad hop, not his fault, just one more example of your peculiar sense of humor which has caused so much hilarity through the ages. I guess what I'm trying to tell you is this: I need to feel hope. I want to believe there's a purpose to all this. That somewhere there's some meaning to the dropped fly balls and the endless hours in the hospital waiting room and the daily dread of getting out of bed. I don't need much, but I need something, a hint, a sign, a quick "thumbs up" from the Home Office. Just once, I need this boy to catch the ball. please. . . . *(To God.)* Thank you.

SCIENCE FAIR
Jeanmarie Williams

Comic
Jethro, sixteen

> *Jethro is presenting his science fair project before a panel of judges.*
> *He has a display of three different broccoli plants, marked "OK,"*
> *"Big," and "Dead." He has a violin.*

JETHRO: Resolved: If you talk nice to broccoli, it will grow better and produce more vitamins and make it more nutritious. For my experiment,
I decided to measure the effect of different qualities of sounds on
three broccoli plants. Broccoli, as you know, or maybe not, well, anyway, broccoli contains an electrical charge, which, if stimulated, pro-
duces better broccoli. Well, like, you couldn't really make a lamp out
of it or anything, I tried that last year, but, OK, if you stimulate it
in the right way it will produce bigger florets, more vitamins . . . Yeah.
So, yeah, this is my broccoli.

> *(He stares out at us. Then he remembers to continue.)*

OK. So here's the thing about it. You should notice that these
plants all look different. One is big and healthy, another is just OK
and the other one is pretty much dead.

> *(Again he stares.)*

Yeah. So, OK. Here's what I did. I maintained my plants in different rooms. I exposed each of my plants to the same words and
tone of voice every day, five times a day. I said different things to each
one, but what I said to each individual plant was the same . . . Yeah,
did you get that? OK, like this is what I said to this one, every day.

> *(He turns to the dead-looking head of broccoli. Jethro turns around*
> *and prepares his character. He turns around and has taken on the per-*
> *sona of a huge, brutish, mean man. He focuses on the dead broccoli. He*
> *drops the character for a moment.)*

OK, so this isn't what I said every day to this one, I mixed it up
a little bit, but this is basically the idea.

(He takes on the character again.)

Yooouuu, stupid worthless piece of crap! You dumbass piece of fiber! Who'd want to eat you anyway? What are you, *green?* Are you green? God damn the day you were born! Die! Die! Die! So, yeah, so this one's dead. And . . . this is what I said to this one: *(He turns to the "OK" looking broccoli.)* Get on Route 7. When you hit Grove Street exit, get in the right lane and bear right at the yield sign. It's a tough merge, so watch out you don't change lanes. At the Mobil station, turn right. Go through three lights and the high school is on your left hand side, just past the Wal-Mart.

This one grew, but it's, you know, just OK. So you got that. Yeah. And so this is what I said to this one.

(He indicates the one marked "Big." It looks beautiful and healthy. He takes out his violin and plays to the plant. It's rather beautiful. He stops and looks at us. Then he starts to play again, as the lights change.)

SEVEN STAGES OF AN AFFAIR

Lorraine Forrest-Turner

Comic
Tony, twenties to forties

Direct address to audience. Tony talks about why men can't seem to be faithful to one woman.

TONY: Why do guys screw around? *(Pause.)* Because they can. Oh, come on, no guy lies on his deathbed thinking "I wish I'd slept with less women." *(Pause.)* Unless of course he's dying of syphilis or something.

OK, maybe that's an oversimplification but I tell you, I have thought about this long and hard and I still haven't come up with a better answer. I've been through it all. "My wife doesn't understand me." "I was denied the breast as a baby." "I am driven by the biological urge to plant my seeds in as many different wombs as possible."

None of them add up. Linda *does* understand me. I was suckled until I was fourteen months old. And I always use a condom.

The trouble with me is I *like* women. No honestly, I really like women. I like the way they look, the way they smell, the way they feel. I like the way they talk, the way they get inside your head and make you feel good about yourself. *(Pause.)* Of course, they also have a habit of making you feel as if you've been caught looking up the teacher's skirt but that's a totally different story. *(Pause.)* No, the way I look at it, spend two hours with some bloke and you come away knowing why Arsenal lost 2-1 and why your pension is worth half what you thought it was. Spend two hours with a beautiful woman and you don't give a toss either way.

No, the big question for me isn't why do guys screw around, it's why do they stop?

SEVEN STAGES OF AN AFFAIR

Lorraine Forrest-Turner

Comic
Tony, twenties to forties

> *Direct address to audience. Tony talks about why men can't seem to be faithful to one woman.*

TONY: *(Slowly, enjoying every second of the memory.)* They get it all wrong you know, women. They think all we want to do is get laid. Not me. Making love to a woman for the first time is like driving to the airport as you head off on holiday. You know, that wonderful expectation, that feeling when you know something new and magical is going to happen but you almost don't want to get there in case this is the best bit. But Caroline was your genuine Carlsberg holiday. A couple of fumbling schoolboys and ten years of routine marriage had made her insatiable. She was so just wonderfully uncomplicated. There was none of that playing grown-ups stuff with its false modesty and points scoring. It was just pure uncomplicated sexual indulgence. And I couldn't get enough of her.

She made me feel good about myself. Like I was good. Like I could achieve anything. She didn't try to control me. Or my life. Didn't hassle me. Didn't ask endless questions about my day. She just enjoyed me, accepted me for what I was.

Yep, life was looking good. I won a couple of biggies, hit target inside a month and made the fastest promotion in living history when my regional manager collapsed and died during our first one-to-one. Shame, nice guy. My mate Eric got us a couple of tickets to the England-Germany match. And Linda stopped having a go at me about being away so much when I agreed to go round the kitchen showrooms with her. All in all, life just couldn't get better.

SORCERESS

Don Nigro

Seriocomic
John Pendragon, fifty-seven

> *In the autumn of 1867, John Pendragon has taken Gavin Rose out
> to the woods to go hunting. Actually they both hate hunting, but
> the women back at the house were driving them crazy, and they
> needed to get away. Gavin is actually John's illegitimate son, which
> Gavin has suspected all his life, but the two have never spoken of
> it. They've been through the Civil War together, are both home now,
> married, and living in the old Pendragon house, and a crisis has
> been precipitated in the household by the return of Gavin's mother,
> a housemaid John seduced, or was seduced by, depending on whose
> version you believe, in his father's library, twenty years ago, and who
> was in fact his own illegitimate half-sister. Now John knows it's time
> to speak with Gavin about these matters, if he's ever going to. But
> he's not a man who finds explanations or the expression of affection
> easy. They're sitting at the campfire in the woods at night.*

JOHN: I stopped trying to figure women out a long time ago.

(Pause.)

Seems like we came through these woods in the war. Hard to
tell. They all kind of bleed together in my head now. Before long
there won't be any woods like this. The stupid sons of bitches will
have cut them all down. Greed. When my father first came out to
Ohio, everything was woods. He had a thing about the trees. Some
old Indian told him it was a curse to cut them down, so he started
building his house around old trees. That's why we've got so many
weird little courtyards and gardens. It made a damned crooked mess
out of the house but it saved some of the old trees. Of course the
house is mostly wood, so he must have cut down something. My father was eccentric in a big way. He was like some sort of demented

god. Couldn't stop making his own nightmare. More and more rooms to walk through. Never enough to hide in. He could talk to himself, but he couldn't talk to me.

(Pause.)

He was right about the trees. I think maybe we got some Druid blood, somewhere back there. Cut down the trees, soil washes away, the land plays out, and everything dies. Starting to happen already. Sometimes, you know, Gavin, you and I have got to sit down and talk about some things.

(Pause.)

Last night I dreamed the colors on the trees began to change. At night you could see this glow like the mold that grows on corpses in the woods. I was walking in woods like this, and I fell over a dead man. His eyes are glowing, like pearls. Shakespeare. I used to sit in my father's library and she would read to me.

(Pause.)

I miss my wife.

(Pause.)

Let's go home.

SUN, STAND THOU STILL
Steven Gridley

Dramatic
Driver, forties

> *The Driver defends himself from a Hitchhiker's accusation that he's
> a casual wanderer.*

DRIVER: Let me show you something. Look at that odometer. See it?
What's it say? Two hundred twelve thousand, four hundred and fifty-
six. I purchased this fine machine with one hundred fifty-four thousand, nine hundred and eighty-seven miles on it. You want to see
the title? Purchased this very truck on this very road. Every mile since
one hundred fifty-four thousand, nine hundred and eighty-seven has
been on this road. Every single one. You good with math? Probably
not. That's almost sixty thousand miles. Been traveling west since I can
remember. Direct and nonstop. You think there's anything casual about
that? Going in one direction? One. There was only one time, one time,
that I stopped heading west. At about the forty thousand-mile mark I
got mixed up. Suddenly wasn't quite sure if I was traveling west anymore. You go forty thousand miles in one direction, your mind starts
to doubt, you know? You expect something to happen, I mean . . .
something. An ocean? I thought maybe my mind had played a trick
on me. That maybe I got turned around and wasn't traveling west
at all but was traveling . . . *(He shudders at the idea.)* I tell you . . .
Just the thought of it . . . I had sweat in my eyes, my hands were
shaking, I had to stop the truck and gather myself. Forty thousand
fucking miles in the wrong direction! I stepped out of the truck with
my head down. Didn't want to see the sun. No sir, I didn't want to
look at the sun 'cause I knew it'd tell me if I was wrong. If I was traveling southeast or . . . *(Again, another shudder.)* Eventually, I got up
the nerve, though. I had to. I looked up and . . . now you're not going
to believe me here, but this is the truth. It's the God's honest truth.

It wasn't moving. It was right above me, perched like a vulture. No shadows, no nothing. It wasn't moving. So I decided to wait until it did move. I sat right on the side of the road and waited. For fifteen hours I waited. Me and the sun, eye to eye, having ourselves a little staring contest. Seeing who'll move first. And I was going to win. I was going to win, Goddamn it, or shrivel up right there, 'cause I couldn't go anywhere without knowing which way was west! I would die first! *(Pause.)* Sure enough, fifteen hours later, the sun started moving again. I was right. Still traveling west. But I think that's what burnt my eyes. You ever hear of something like that?

TEN UNKNOWNS
John Robin Baitz

Dramatic
Judd, twenties

> *Judd, a rising young painter, has been working as an assistant to a famous painter named Raphelson, whom he here confronts.*

JUDD: I don't want to be dead, I just want . . .

    . . . I just want one thing. To know why? *(Beat.)* Why on earth did you do this to me? Look at me. This is what you've done. *(Beat. Totally articulate and clear-headed. He goes on, shaking his head, still baffled.)* Why? Malcolm. The public nature of it. As soon as there were other people to witness this — you turned — The satisfaction. You made fun of me with Trevor, to my face, and worse, with her too. Any opportunity for indignity, humiliation: "Cabbages for hands," erasure, rewriting history to your own specs . . . why? All the things you hated. The prospect of New York. Of what you would do to me — as a retrospective, in a gallery. Yow. I can imagine it — your constant digs and with so many people there — I don't understand it. I don't. Can you please try and explain it. *(Beat. Judd is in tears. He shakes his head.)* I'm sorry if I . . . *(Beat.)* Did something — if I seemed — disrespectful or . . . *(Beat. There is silence. Judd tries to pull himself together. . . . He shakes his head.)* — I keep trying to figure out why you would possibly want to do this and I can't even — *(Beat.)* I wasn't around for all the years you watched yourself become invisible and more and more marginal . . . It must have been . . . *(He stops. He nods. Suddenly clear to him.)* I know what it is. *(Beat. Simply amazed.)* Take my work — sell it . . . and sell it as your own — and you get your revenge on everyone — me — because I can actually paint — and these people whom you loathe, who did this to you. It's so malignant. It's brilliant and twisted. You get everything you want. That's what it is. Revenge on all of us. *(Pause.)*

You're a comic book villain, do you know that, Malcolm? And in case you hadn't noticed — up there — back in New York, they've declared that painting is dead. You have no idea how tiny the stakes are. *(Judd is suddenly absolutely certain and direct and compelled.)* But you know who I am? I am a mute with great feeling, huge battles going on inside, storms, plagues . . . but no way to express any of it. These useless skills. To execute a . . . but otherwise impotent, nothing else. *(Beat.)* I loved you Malcolm, I would sit here and understand exactly what you wanted, what you were trying to do. Just a nod or a shake or twitch from you was enough. Fantastic. Magic. Collaboration, the sum bigger than the parts, I was never better, you were never braver — and however it worked — when we were together, something great — But then, alone, when I went off, I went through pad after pad, now I was fucked . . . but all of it a blur, worthless. Dead. Nothing to say. Torn paper.

THIS THING OF DARKNESS
Craig Lucas and David Schulner

Dramatic
Abbey, twenty-two

> *Abbey, recently graduated from college, is here talking to his college
> roommate, Donald, who has come to visit.*

ABBEY: I ran out of pills, Sunday a week ago, my prescription had expired,
I got all wrapped up in finals and all-nighters, I guess you're not supposed to do that. I mean, Christ, I was on Ritalin from, what, seven?,
and these since they started making them. And . . . sitting there in
that medieval gown — what is that? I mean, any graduation cere-
mony, just in design is completely frightening. Foucault talks about
this thing called a penopticon. . . .

The first page. It's like a physical structure — the way prisons
are set up, or courthouses. One focal point, everybody in rows; it
creates discipline. And this — I mean, the heat, humidity, the way
we were lined up with literally thousands of people watching us —
and of course I still picked out my mother crying. I've been in school
since I could remember being alive, and now it's over? So essentially,
life as I know it was over. And, OK, I was like hearing voices. . . .

I know I know. I mean, not like Joan of Arc, they weren't saying "Find the dauphin!" they were saying, "You suck you suck you
suck." If ever there was a time I needed my pills; I felt like we were
all being pushed out of a plane, and instead of a parachute we were
given these little pieces of paper with a ribbon on them, and I was
practically last, so I had hours of watching friends plummet to the
ground as they got their Diplomas of Death. "Here, go into the world
and die, as we have not prepared you for anything except memoriz-
ing your social security number and being in debt." . . .

By the time they got to the T's I had bitten off all my finger-
nails and didn't stop until I felt something hard against my teeth. . . .

You were having fun. I heard my name, I swear I thought my life was over. That's why I walked so slowly, hoping to regain some . . . I don't know, then someone reached for my diploma, the dean went white — *my* hands? And . . . seeing that, I . . . *puked* on her, front row, bloody fucking vomit all over Monica Agualisi's hair and gown. I saw her pulling it out of her eyelashes as I passed out. So of course I'm going to grad school, that makes sense. I'm not ready for my life. And there's not much else I can do with a philosophy degree.

THROW PITCHFORK
Alexander Thomas

Dramatic
Jimmy, twenties to forties

> *Jimmy is the eldest son of an abusive alcoholic. Here, he could ei-*
> *ther be explaining his heroin use to another junkie, or to a rehab*
> *counselor. Jimmy could be any age range from early twenties to as*
> *old as forty. He is a heroin junkie. He is the oldest brother of four*
> *boys. He was written as a Black man but there is no reason he could*
> *not be any other ethnicity.*

ADMIT IT

JIMMY: *(Lanky, dangling arms and fingers. Head turning from side to side*
like some nervous radar.) I'm an addict. A junkie. I admit that. I admit
that. I get sick and tired of people talking. "Look at Jimmy. Jimmy
is the oldest one. Jimmy's supposed to be the big brother — he mess-
ing up. Jimmy supposed to help his little brothers — he running the
streets. Jimmy supposed to set an example — he shootin' dope." He
"dippin' n' dabbin'," he "selling n' dealing," he "boostin' n' stealin'."
Hey, I'm *gonna do some horse!* I admit that. I'm gonna boast a little,
steal a little. But at least I admit it. I'll take something from you but
it's to feed my habit. It's not malicious. It's not to do you harm. I
ain't never hurt nobody. And I'm gonna always, as soon I can, pay
it back. You will git your shit back soon as I can. So I don't really
see what the problem is. I know it's wrong but I admit that. I tried
to stop. I been to treatment. Programs n' things. Shit don't work for
me. All the lingo: I got a "disease," an "obsession," a "compulsion."
I gotta "arrest it a day at a time." I got "enablers." Come from a "dys-
functional family." Now, that's true! That's true. This family? Like,
just put your self in this situation. Just imagine this. Let's say you
got a brother that you know is a junkie, an addict. Now, you know

that this brother has been messin' around shootin' up Since he was what, seventeen, eighteen, maybe even younger. Now just imagine this. You let this brother stay at your house. Now, you know he's been known to steal, borrow, whatever from time to time when he needs to get high. Now, you leave a credit card laying around. A credit card! It's not in your purse, not in your wallet, not in drawer. Nowhere. No normal safe place. It's on the table. Just laying on the table! He takes and uses it. Any junkie would do this, right? Now, would you call the police on your own blood? See . . . "Dysfuntional!" Call the police on your own blood. I'm not sayin' I'm not wrong. I am wrong, I am wrong. I admit that. All I'm sayin' is I get sick and tired, and I'm sick and tired of being sick and tired, of this family doing stupid shit and then blame it on me when I'm just being an addict. A junkie, that's all. And that, I admit.

THE TRANSPARENCY OF VAL

Stephen Belber

Comic
Rheum, any age

> *Mr. Rheum is a college professor, here welcoming Our Hero, Val,
> to school.*

RHEUM: Hi there, Val, welcome to our school
I'm here to teach you logic and a slice of Golden Rule
Certain things your parents said are quite completely wrong
I'll now correct just some of them, with my little song
As to all this nonsense apropos "Thou shalt not kill"
Survival of the fittest seems to put that all to nil
We kill each other daily, it's a form of re-baptism
But all of it is legal because it's called cap-i-ta-lism
And as for that big lie that in the beginning there was light
I'd like to set the record straight by stating it was night
Nothingness was ruler and around it darkness hung
The concept of humanity had yet to have begun
Our humble little universe was just an ole black hole
Until the Big Bang came along to set us on a roll
. . . Any questions?
    Well of course there's peace on earth, good will toward man, man
bites dog, the dog ate my homework, eight minutes for light to get
to Earth, light is energy, energy makes us sexually active, it's good
to be sexually active so long as your mother's not making your bed.
One has to cut the cord. On that note, don't sleep with your mothers, no matter how tempting; girls same with your fathers, boys same
with your fathers, girls — go ahead and sleep with Mom, the rest
of us find that kinky. Speaking of Oedipal urges — our society is
based on the irresistible impetus of profit motive which is really just

a polite way of saying, "Love me, Mother, love me," but profit is legal and mother boinking's not so we have to watch our step. In addition, we hold these truths to be self-evident: "Just do it," "Get it while you can," "Good will toward Mom: — Hey but seriously! — As for fathers — certain of you will feel guilty — as you grow — for the things they did and the evil they bequeathed you; you'll read history, be spat at, see the light and recover memories. All of that's to be expected — for fathers are the essential source of all bigotry and greed in this world. I'm just here to reinforce that. By the way, America doesn't play favorites when it comes to religion, meaning the municipal crèche must cost the same as the municipal menorah. As for the Muslims — nice folks but too much Jihad, not enough Ramadan; Jehovah's Witnesses — pretty damn kooky but good job on not saluting the flag. *(Muttering.)* Fucking commies. OK! — have a nice night and don't believe everything your parents tell you, especially that one about Abraham and Isaac, because the fact is, the Abe-man was ready to annihilate that old biblical favorite "Thou shalt not kill." Talk about a mixed message from Dad. Can't have your cake and kill your son. Just goes to show you, who woulda thunk! OK — off you go!

THE TRANSPARENCY OF VAL
Stephen Belber

Comic
Sebum, forties to fifties

Sebum is an eccentric college professor, here addressing his class.

SEBUM: It's bullshit, it's bullshit
   Everything you've learned, up to now
   It's horseshit, it's donkey-ass-shit
   If you thought it was a lion, it's really just a cow
   Hey you sittin' there with that hope upon your face
   If you think that life is simple you must be from outer space
   Now that you're in college, there are things you must explore
   Roosevelt had a mistress, and Kennedy was a whore

   But that's really just the surface of the knowledge you'll receive
   For the point of higher learning is to doubt what you perceive
   Here's one more example that you really ought to know
   Lincoln freed the slaves as a political sideshow
   And on the topic of revision, let us look a bit more near
   For if God is so damn gentle, why are humans full of fear?
   Which brings us to Kierkegaard's *Fear and Trembling*, which, as you know, deals with the story of Abraham and Isaac. A man *commanded* by God to sacrifice his son so as to demonstrate his faith. Now sure, there are those who say that by pulling a double-edged saber on his own flesh and blood, Abraham screwed his son up for life. "Hey, Dad, I'm your son, not the family goat." But what *I'm* saying is — the man *acted* on his beliefs. He may have been a chump, he may have screwed up his son, he may even have believed in a God that doesn't exist, but the fact is, he *did* what he thought was *right*. And I dig that. I really do, I dig the hell out of it.

TWILIGHT:
LOS ANGELES, 1992
Anna Deavere Smith

Dramatic
Charles Lloyd, forties to fifties

> *Lloyd is a lawyer for an Asian woman accused of killing a black child during the L.A. Riots*

CHARLES LLOYD
Attorney for Soon Ja Du

Again, a very verbal man, a gift for talking — speaking rapidly, with expression, an argument, a plea.

CHARLES LLOYD: How am I a sellout?
How am I an Uncle Tom?
A lot of this is just plain old jealousy.
I learned that as a child.
Whoever had the money in town.
Doctors, morticians,
It's like actresses.
People say that actresses are fickle!
I haven't found actresses to be any more fickle than anyone else.
And you have that going with lawyers.
"What looks good on a lawyer?
That's black and brown?"
"A doberman
A vicious doberman!"
"Why won't a snake bite a lawyer?" —
"Professional courtesy."
"What does a lawyer do when he dies?"
"He lies still!"

Now this lady accosted a child for shoplifting
How is that a political case?
Let's read the ballistics report into the record.
"A hair trigger"
(He stops and responds to a question from the author.)
A hair trigger?
That's an expression from the Old West.
It's something men know a lot more about than women.
" . . . external examination
has revealed evidence
of disassembly
the-wrong-screws-were-reassembled
dry-firing-of-this-weapon-reveals-that-the-hammer
can-be-pushed-off
without — pulling — the trigger!
Hitting the hammer in full cock
will discharge this firearm without pulling the trigger.
This firearm must be classified as
unsafe!"
They *made* it political!
If Latasha had been killed by a black woman it wouldn't have ever been
in the black the papers,
it's such a common occurrence!

WTC VIEW

Brian Sloan

Dramatic
Alex, midtwenties

> *Alex, who works on Wall Street, tells where he was and what he
> saw on September 11, 2001.*

ALEX: I had an early meeting that morning to go over some new bonds.
The meeting ended around quarter of nine and — . . .

I was in the sky lobby and everyone was getting off the eleva-
tors, going to work. So I got in an empty elevator by myself and hit
the lobby button. And I'm just standing there, whistling and looking at my feet . . . you know, elevator stuff. Then suddenly the whole
thing comes to a stop and there's this huge whoosh of air then a low
rumbling sound. And the lights and everything flicker off for a
minute but then come back on. I tried to open the doors but they
were stuck. And then I heard some voices coming from the speaker
but it was all jumbled. Then there was another rumbling sound, not
as big. After that I was beginning to think this is probably pretty serious but still I didn't know what was going on. A voice comes on
the speaker that I can finally understand and says there's a fire and
that someone's coming to get me. So I just stand there waiting. So I
wait and wait and wait. No one comes. All I can see is this sliver of
dusty light through the doors and I think maybe I should try to open
them again. So I did and they opened. Just like that. I couldn't believe
it but all that time I was in the lobby. On the ground floor. So I walk
out and look around and all the windows are smashed and there's
all this smoke but there are no people. I mean *no one* is around. So
I walk out to the plaza and there is just — all this . . . luggage. Suitcases
that are open and garment bags and business clothes and shoes . . . so
many pairs of shoes. Then I hear this huge thump behind me — almost like a mini-explosion. And about twenty feet away is what I guess

is a body . . . not 'cause it looks like one. But because of all the blood. So I look up and see two more coming down, holding up tablecloths as these makeshift parachutes that would work for a few seconds and then . . . don't. At that point I knew I should run but with all this carnage and things falling I didn't know where to go. I froze. Then, outta nowhere, I feel something on my wrist — something's that burning hot. I think I'm on fire for a minute, that some piece of something's hit me, but I turn around and there's this huge fireman grabbing me by the wrist and he starts running, dragging me behind him. I tried to slow down and turn around and see exactly what the hell's going on but the fireman yells "Don't turn around." And hearing that . . . I just get shivers all over my body. So we're just booking — down Fulton, over to West Street. Even though we're running, I feel cold all of a sudden. The only part of my body that feels warm is my wrist where he's holding me, and it's really starting to hurt. Finally, we get to the river where all these fireboats are parked and I hear this enormous crack, like a clap of thunder. I turn around to see it falling — coming down into this insane cloud that starts barreling toward us. The fireman just throws me on a fireboat but the cloud stops before it gets to us. So I'm sitting on the boat and just shaking . . . I'm so cold. And a nurse comes up to me, staring at me, and asks if I'm hurt and I look at my pants and there's all this blood but it's not mine — it's from the plaza. So she checks me out and I'm not hurt at all. Not a scratch. The only thing I had was this big bruise on my wrist from the fireman. From his grip. That's all.

WTC VIEW
Brian Sloan

Dramatic
Max, twenty

Max tells where he was and what he saw on September 11, 2001.

MAX: I mean I was walking down Sixth Avenue, heading to my nine o'clock. The first plane buzzed right over me. I looked up because it was so loud and knew something was totally wrong. And then I followed it and saw it go right into the Trade Center. I mean . . . right into the building. And that thing had flown right over my head . . . *(Beat.)* This is kinda weird but . . . last summer I went to check out that movie *Pearl Harbor* with a couple of friends of mine. It was totally stupid — Ben Affleck as some flying ace. Gimme a break. But there was this one scene where the Japanese planes are flying past a bunch of kids playing baseball. And I remember thinking how intense that must have been to be one of those kids. To see history flying right over your head . . . and when I was watching the movie I thought, damn, nothing that serious or historical is ever gonna happen to me. And then, two months later . . . there I am on Sixth Avenue looking up. *(A heavy beat.)* And now I feel like, I don't know, like I almost wished something like that to happen. I know I didn't really, but . . . it's what I wanted in a way. To be part of history and now I'm in it all the way.

101